You and
Your Child

by Charles R. Swindoll

SENIOR PASTOR, FIRST EVANGELICAL FREE CHURCH
FULLERTON, CALIFORNIA

THOMAS NELSON PUBLISHERS
Nashville   New York

Tenth printing

Library of Congress Cataloging in Publication Data

Swindoll, Charles R
    You and your child.

    Includes bibliographical references.
    1. Children—Management.   2. Family—Religious life.
I. Title.
HQ769.S963   649'.1   77–1692
ISBN 0–8407–5118–4
ISBN 0–8407–5616–X pbk.

To CYNTHIA, my "fruitful vine"
and to CURTIS, CHARISSA, COLLEEN, and CHUCK
our four "olive plants"
I affectionately dedicate
the contents of this book
as well as the rest of my life

Contents

Foreword

With the obvious crumbling of the foundations of the American home so easily visible today, thousands of young mothers and fathers are begging for help. The siren song of the secular prophets who lured a whole generation into moral and spiritual bankruptcy in the sixties is too vivid in memory to attract many today. As a result the trusted and ancient wisdom of the Scriptures is now enjoying a new popularity.

But the expounders of the ancient wisdom today are a new breed of cats as compared to the writers of Christian books for the home a quarter century ago. They are no longer content with a kind of sloganeering ("Wives, submit yourselves to your own husbands;" "Children, obey your parents") but take the time patiently to explain and describe. They no longer exude a faintly sneering air of condemnation for those who already are caught up in deep problems, but are humble and honest about their own possibilities for failure. They do not dodge the real and sticky problems, but, in the name of the living God, they take firm hold of the witches and ogres that cause domestic unrest.

Chuck Swindoll is the best of the breed. I shall forever be grateful to him for having laid to rest (I hope for all time) the dangerous myths that have plagued thousands because of the mistranslated verse: "Bring up a child in the way he should go, and when he is old he will not depart from it." This book brings us face to face with fresh views of old verses that will open the eyes of many to their real meanings. With candor and humor he makes the Scriptures speak to our times and our problems, and that is the business of a Christian expositor above all else.

Ray C. Stedman

INTRODUCTION

There is a well-worn path stretching across every life. It is impossible to grow up without traveling down that path. To retrace our steps, reviewing the sights and sounds that emerge from the time tunnel, often brings the sting of pain and the struggle of confusion. Why? Because that path is strewn with piles of litter.

I am referring to the path of *childhood*.

How seldom we adults enjoy satisfying scenes as we walk through the museum of our memories! It makes little difference that we were born into a home of great wealth and cultural sophistication or into a family that lacked the finer things of life. Nor is it highly significant whether we were raised as a youngster in the same house throughout our childhood in a quiet midwestern town or near the pounding surf of the Pacific Ocean, or whether we moved a dozen or more times during our formative years. Happiness and contentment are not the by-products of economy or geography. The measure of our pleasure is *people*—the relationships sustained with our parents (or guardians) and with the other members of our family.

This book deals with that issue. Since the job of clearing away the debris from this path rests essentially with parents, it is a book for moms and dads . . . those of us engaged in the exacting and often frustrating task of raising children. If you are like me, you are weary of theories and seminars and sermons and opinions that sound good but prove unrealistic.

What we want is reliable direction, useful and dependable principles *that work*. We long to do what is right and best for our children. Our great goal is to launch into society secure, mature, confident, capable young adults who can handle the pressures thrown at them in the demanding arena of life. The cutting edge of that process is the home—not the school or the church. It is in the home that the rubber meets the road. It is there that our children are prepared for the arena.

The book you are holding in your hand was spawned in a very common crucible, a busy (occasionally hectic) home. It was nurtured in the daily (occasionally painful) process of raising four active children, two hamsters, one guinea pig, one rabbit, and a miniature Schnauzer named Heidi . . . not to mention a continual stream of neighborhood, church, and school friends too numerous to mention.

Like you, we have endured several surgeries, broken bones, sucked thumbs, bouts with the flu, diaper rashes, braces on teeth, temper tantrums, wet beds, crying spells, sleepless nights, spilled milk, dog messes, football practices, piano lessons, allergy shots, car pools, bathtub rings, mounds of ironing, folding socks, making lunches, singing songs, attending church, and most of all *laughing*. The very fact this volume was ever written is a minor miracle.

Besides my lovely wife, I have four people in mind who deserve special thanks.

I am grateful to my friend, Dr. Joe Temple of Abilene, Texas, for passing on to me his keen insights in raising children. With his approval, I share in my first two chapters some of the truths he has now put into print in his book, *Know Your Child*.[1] I appreciate his publisher, Baker Book House, allowing me to use and build upon some of Dr. Temple's original thoughts.

Equal thanks goes to Dr. Howard Hendricks, my major professor during my days at Dallas Theological Seminary. Germs from his course on "The Christian Home" infected me with the right disease . . . and his life has convinced me that one can actually practice what he preaches.

I am also indebted to Peter Gillquist of Thomas Nelson for his invaluable, enthusiastic assistance in the relentless process of putting into print the content of these pages.

And to my personal secretary, Helen Peters, who invested untold hours typing (and retyping) the manuscripts, I express my profound appreciation.

One final thought is in order. This book's major source of information comes from the One who originated the whole idea of the home and the family . . . God Himself. I have simply taken some of the truths He has preserved for us in the Old and New

Testaments and applied them to the task of raising children today.

If you find ideas or suggestions that encourage you or give you an increased depth of insight into your children, God gets all the glory. After all, He is the One Who has brought you and your child together and provides you with the daily wisdom you need to raise your child successfully.

Charles R. Swindoll

1
Mom and Dad . . .
Meet Your Child

Six million Americans will take a life-changing step this year. Not only will this step change their lives, it will have a profound effect on the next generation as well.

They will have children.

How they raise these youngsters will have a greater impact on society than the way they vote, the art they create, the books they read, the technological problems they solve, or the planets they visit in space. And yet, perhaps never before in our nation's history have parents faced and felt more pressure or sought more professional help in the rearing of their children.

In one of America's leading publications[2] Kenneth Woodward and Phyllis Malamud revealed the results of their study and analysis of our domestic scene. These are the issues with which parents must cope. The scene is both complex and depressing, a rather unattractive setting for a tiny tot to begin his life.

To conserve time and space, I'll summarize their initial observations:

1. *Finances*. The cost of bearing, clothing, feeding, entertaining, and educating children is the greatest in our history.

2. *Working mothers*. For the first time ever, a majority of American mothers hold jobs outside the home, many out of necessity rather than desire.

3. *Public opinion*. Respect for parenthood as a vocation is rapidly declining in our land. Questions like "Is having kids really worth the sacrifice?" and "If you had it to do over, would you have children?" are frequently being asked.

4. *Objectives*. Relatively few people agree about what "good parents" should do or what a child should be like when he becomes a young adult. Ultimate objectives are unclear.

5. *Divorce*. In 1974 the parents of more than one million children were divorced. That's twice the number of a decade

before. A curious fact is that an increasing number of fathers are gaining custody of children after divorce proceedings are final. However, in many cases neither parent wants the children.

6. *Drugs and alcohol.* Teen-age drug abuse and alcoholism are on the rise. An alarming number of pre-teens are involved in both.

7. *Death.* The second leading cause of death among individuals between ages *fifteen* and *twenty-four* is now suicide.

8. *Crime.* Juvenile delinquency is rapidly rising to epidemic proportions. One child in nine can be expected to appear in juvenile court before he turns *eighteen*.

9. *Runaways.* The statistics are grim, revealing that at least one million children (most from middle-class families) run away each year, some never returning.

10. *Abuse.* Child battering, gross neglect, incest, and parental abandonment are increasing, becoming a serious public health problem without satisfactory answers. Child abuse is now the second leading cause of death among those between birth and twelve years of age.

11. *Illegitimacy.* Despite the ready availability of birth-control devices and abortion services, the rate of illegitimate births among adolescents continues to climb. By age *eighteen*, one out of ten American girls (married or unmarried), is a mother—*and* a prime candidate for increasing the syndrome of divorce, abuse, delinquency, and neglect.

12. *No time.* Even mothers who stay home don't necessarily spend time with their children. Few children eat dinner regularly with their parents. Television, peer groups, outside-the-home activities, and school involvements occupy the child's time far more than do his parents.

It's a bleak, tragic scene. Yet, six million Americans will join the ranks this year, becoming either part of the answer or part of the problem.

So much for sad statistics . . . let's get specific.

You may soon be among the six million. Perhaps you already are. You are concerned. Your concern is neither passive nor hidden. If it were you would have never picked up this book. You are anxious to do the right thing—you're just not sure what that is. Those necessary directions are fuzzy, maybe absent altogether. Opinions and philosophies have failed.

Let's start with something very basic. Turning our focus from the discouraging morass of society's problems (they will always be there), we want to spend the rest of this book on one major, all-important relationship: that vital relationship between you and your child.

In the remainder of this first chapter I'd like to introduce that child to you. Strange as it may seem, mom and dad, *I want you to meet your child!* Most parents I have met are trying to raise the little people who live under their roofs, have the same last names, and eat their food—yet they do not really know them.

I suggest the place to begin is with a single ingredient. Every parent who wants to know his child must possess it. It is not a high I.Q. nor is it plenty of money. It is neither an understanding of psychological principles nor a strong religious background. The single ingredient most needed is *sensitivity*. A parent who is genuinely sensitive to his child will generally have little difficulty coming to know his child.

My children pulled a fast one on me last Christmas. They teamed up, pooled their vast financial resources, and bought me a small, framed motto to put on my desk. It read:

DIETS ARE FOR PEOPLE
WHO ARE THICK . . . AND TIRED OF IT

At first it made me thmile. Then I got thad. Especially when I realized I wasn't thick of being thick!

There is another thickness, however, far more serious than physical thickness. It is *parental* thickness . . . being out of touch, unaware, lacking insight and perception. In one word, it is insensitivity. By "parental thickness" I mean the common problem of tuning our children out, being dull, preoccupied, insensitive to their makeup and their needs.

Dr. James Dobson, in his fine book *Hide or Seek* emphasizes the importance of building self-esteem into our children. As he develops a strategy for reaching that objective, he presents five barriers that can cause a child to doubt his worth. The first barrier he lists is parental insensitivity.[3]

Strange as it may sound, you can give birth to a child, nurse the child, clothe, feed, discipline, and educate that child—without really *knowing* the one you are raising. It is not that you lack exposure. Untold hours are spent in one another's presence. What is missing then? What is the answer? Sensitivity. We parents must somehow strip away the mental thickness that hinders the process of coming to know the child we hold in our arms and put to bed night after night.

Knowing your child is primary. Loving your child requires knowing that child. Face it: it is impossible to love someone you don't know. And that includes your own child! If that is true of loving, it is equally true of training. No parent can expect to train a child correctly if he doesn't really know the one being trained. The effectiveness of training your child is in direct proportion to the extent you know your child.

Tucked away in the Old Testament is a book of wise, insightful sayings—Proverbs by name. Most of these proverbs were written by Solomon, a man of incredible wisdom in practical, everyday life. In Prov. 22:6, we find a very familiar verse most Christians can quote from memory:

> Train up a child in the way he should go,
> Even when he is old he will not depart from it.

Let's probe this well-known saying for the next few minutes. Read it over once again, just to make sure you are seeing what is written.

Some contemporary religious interpretations would paraphrase the verse: "Be sure your child is in Sunday school and church regularly. Cement into his mind a few memorized verses from the Bible plus some hymns and prayers. Send him to Christian camps during the summers of his formative years, and certainly, if at all possible, place the child in a Christian school so he can be educated by people whose teaching is based on the Bible. Because, after all, someday he will sow his wild oats. For sure, he will have his fling. But when he gets old enough to get over his fling, he will come back to God."

I don't know about you, but that doesn't bring much encouragement to this parent! It doesn't seem to be much of a divine promise: when he is old and decrepit, finished with his fling, he'll come back to God. Big deal! What parent is really motivated to train his child, knowing he's training a prodigal who will ultimately turn against his parents and not return to the Lord until his later years?

Not only is that not much of a promise—it isn't true. You and I can name people forced by sheer determination on the part of strict parents to be in church every Sunday, to read the Bible consistently, to memorize portions of Scripture, to attend camp and Christian school. They went into rebellion as soon as they were launched from their home (often before) and are still in that state, having never returned to the "training" they first experienced.

I can recall a couple of childhood friends who not only rebelled, but died in their rebellion. They never did return to God.

That is no promise at all, and I am convinced it is not what the verse is saying. The book of Proverbs, of course, was originally penned in the Hebrew language. Invariably, things are lost in the process of translation that must be recovered by a study of the original text. So allow me to dig back into the Hebrew tongue to help bring some understanding and color to what is being said.

First of all, what is meant by *train up*? You may be surprised to know the original root word is the term for "the palate, the roof of the mouth, the gums." In verb form, it is the term used for breaking and bringing into submission a wild horse by a rope in the mouth.

The term was also used in the days of Solomon to describe the action of a midwife who, soon after helping deliver a child, would dip her finger into the juice of chewed or crushed dates, reach into the mouth of the infant, and massage the gums and the palate within the mouth so as to create a sensation of sucking, a sense of taste. The juice was also believed to be a cleansing agent in the newborn's mouth. Then she would place the child in its mother's arms to begin feeding from the mother's breast. So it is the word used to describe "developing a thirst."

As time went by, this word for "bringing into submission" and "developing a thirst" came to be known as *dedicate, consecrate.* All of that is involved in *train up*. Let's keep that in mind as we go on.

Train up a *child* . . . I want to stop here for a moment, because when we read the word *child* we invariably think of a little one between the time of infancy and ages four or five. But it's more than that.

The Hebrew word *child* in 1 Sam. 4:21 refers to a newborn infant. But 1 Sam. 1:27 refers to a young boy who had just been weaned. Genesis 21:16 uses the same word for Ishmael in his pre-teen years. Genesis 37:2 uses the same word for Joseph when he was seventeen. Genesis 34:19 uses the word for a young man ready for marriage.

This term *child* is broad. It covers all the years the child is under the roof of the parent, every age from infancy to young adulthood. The entire time is called the period of being "trained up."

Train up, create a thirst in, build into the child the experience of submission (as you would train a horse that had been wild)—a child of all ages in the realm of the home—*in the way he should go.* As you read those words, perhaps you might assume, "I know in my mind the right way for that child to go. I'm the parent and therefore I know what he is to be. So I will set out to train him accordingly, so his life will fit what I know is right. I will apply the same kind of training to each of my children in the same way, because they are all to go in the same way."

At first glance, Prov. 22:6 would seem to deny the idea of individuality. But I want you to know it is just the opposite. Here's why.

Train up a child *in* . . . The term *in* means "in keeping with," "in cooperation with," "in accordance to" the way he should go. In fact, in the New American Standard Bible you will notice verse 6 is margined with the literal rendering "according to his way." That's altogether different from *your* way. God is not saying, "Bring up a child as *you* see him." Instead, He says, "If you want your training to be godly and wise, observe your child, be sensitive and alert so as to discover *his* way, and adapt your training accordingly. In Prov. 30:18-19, the same word for "way" is used as in Prov. 22:6. *Way* is a Hebrew word that suggests the idea of "characteristic," "manner," "mode." Look at the example, Prov. 30:18-19:

There are three things which are too wonderful for me, Four which I do not understand: The way of an eagle in the sky, The way of a serpent on a rock, The way of a ship in the middle of the sea, And the way of a man with a maid.

In each case, *way* is not a specific, well-defined, narrow road or path. It is a characteristic. The one who wrote this verse is saying, "As I observe these four things, I find myself intrigued. I can't put it all together. There is a beautiful coordination, an intriguing mystery which keeps me and captures my attention." *Way* is used in that same sense back in Prov. 22:6—train up a child in keeping with his characteristics.

Now let's dig a little deeper. Both Ps. 7:12 and 11:2 use the same word, *way*, to describe an archer with his bow and arrows. Psalm 11:2 describes the wicked bending the bow before they let the arrow fly to the target. *Bent* or *bending* the bow is the same word in verb form translated *way* in Prov. 22:6. Read a paraphrase of this verse from the Amplified Bible. It catches the meaning correctly: "Train up a child in the way he should go (and in keeping with his individual gift or bent), and when he is old he will not depart from it."

In every child God places in our arms, there is a *bent*, a set of characteristics already established. The bent is fixed and determined before he is given over to our care. The child is not, in fact, a pliable piece of clay. He has been set; he has been bent. And the parents who want to train this child correctly will discover that bent!

You probably have in your home more than one child—perhaps several. Or maybe you were from a home with several children. Were they all alike? (You're smiling!)

I'll tell you, the Swindoll family couldn't be more diverse. We're all active, involved, and opinionated . . . but besides that we're just as different as we can be.

Your family is probably the same way. One of you is creative; another is aggressive, practical. One of you may be very intelligent. Another may be rather nonacademic. Some may be very interested in technical things. Others may be dreamers. For some, life is simple and happy, but for others it is complicated and serious.

What does the unwise parent say? "We're going to get this home in shape. We're going to have everybody fit my mold." The father often leads the way and sets the course of action. Sort of a shape-up-or-ship-out dogmatism. The child hears this and plans to ship out as soon as possible. Why? Because the parent attempts to determine the way of the child. *And that's not for the parents to do.* The parent who is wise and sensitive comes to know the way God made the child, then fits his training accordingly.

Adam and Eve started out with two sons. One was Cain; the other was Abel. Cain was what we would call irreligious—a godless man. Abel, from the same home and the same environment, was just as different from Cain as night from day. Abel was a believer, interested in and sensitive to spiritual things. Although Cain and Abel were brothers, they were opposites.

Jacob and Esau not only were from the same family, they were twins! Jacob was holding onto the heel of his brother as they were born. They were inseparably linked in their mother's womb. That's twins. But as you study Jacob you find he was something of a sissy. In contrast, Esau was a manly, hairy hunter. All the way through their lives, these two men were different. Why? They were bent by God in different ways.

Absalom and Solomon were the same way. They had the same father, the same court life in David's home, yet Absalom was a rebel. Solomon, on the other hand, was a diplomatic man of peace—brilliant and wise.

I think there are two major mistakes dads often make, and I can say this only for dads, because I simply will never be a mother.

First of all, we frequently use the *identical approach* with all our children.

Secondly, we *compare.*

"Susie, how come you're not like Sally?"

"Because I'm not Sally," Susie answers.

"Why not?" Dad says. "Sally is interested in God and His Word. She is sensitive and loves the Lord. Why are you so rebellious?"

"Because I'm Susie."

Dad gets a bigger stick, determined he's going to make her just like her sister. He thinks Susie is talking back. But she is actually struggling to make a very important point. She longs for her dad (or mom) to realize she is totally different from Sally.

Now don't jump to the conclusion that I am suggesting Sally or Susie be allowed to run independently of their parents. I am simply saying it is unwise to compare the two and try to fit them into the same box. That's where the trouble starts.

Think about your past. Go back to that childhood path you once walked. Chances are you began to have serious conflicts with your parents when you sensed they did not understand you, right? And to make matters worse, they compared you with a brother or sister or close friend who was "bent" differently. This only widened the gap in your relationship.

Several years ago my wife and I began to consider the ways we were failing to implement these principles of individuality in the raising of our children. We realized, for example, that we reviewed their report cards several times a year in front of everyone in the family. How unwise! Only the academically gifted child enjoys such an experience. So we implemented a new procedure that works beautifully. Each report card is reviewed alone with the child who brings it home. Each child is encouraged or challenged individually by mom and/or dad, according to his unique level of ability and God-given "bent" . . . not according to how a brother or sister might have done. For the last several years, our children have had no idea what grades one another has made at school. Two benefits have occurred.

First, the children look forward to these personal evaluation sessions with us instead of dreading an embarrassing encounter in front of everyone. Second, individualized suggestions can be given by mom or dad that help strengthen our one-on-one relationship. Children long to have personalized attention from their parents . . . even if it's a report card that draws them together!

Let me make one more comment regarding Prov. 22:6. The verse ends, " . . . when he is old he will not depart from it." The word *old* means "hair on the chin." I understand the literal Hebrew is "bearded one."

Now a man doesn't start growing a beard when he is ninety. He begins to grow a beard when he is approaching maturity. The promise is that when your child reaches maturity, when he is ready to leave home, he will not depart from his training. It's not a promise concerning people ninety years old. It's a promise for those who, having been trained correctly, are leaving the nest and entering into maturity.

Two questions bounce off these pages and probably make you frown in confusion: How can I discover the God-given design of my child? And, once I know how to discover it, what do I look for . . . what are the "bents"?

I'll answer the first one now. The second is much more

involved, and will be answered in the next chapter.

Let's consider one other passage from the book of Proverbs.

It is by his deeds that a lad distinguishes himself if his conduct is pure and right. The hearing ear and the seeing eye, the Lord has made both of them (Prov. 20:11-12).

Obviously, there is no crystal ball for parents. But just as God has given your child built-in characteristics, He has given you your senses. This passage mentions two of them—hearing and seeing. Furthermore, Scripture says your child *distinguishes* himself ("makes himself known") by his deeds or actions.

As you observe and listen, you will discover your child. You will come to know that child. As he acts and reacts, walks and talks, obeys and disobeys, you will have sufficient information to work with him. But you must pay attention! As a parent, you cannot afford the luxury of simply housing, feeding, clothing, and educating your offspring.

A friend of mine has suggested, "Make a study of your child." Wise advice. We, as parents, have a homework assignment from God that will take years to complete. We are assigned the responsibility of coming to know our child. And what we observe and hear must not be ignored. We are to draw upon that information as we train him or her.

It is helpful to remember that your child will not often understand himself. He will look to you to help clear away the fog. He will appreciate your passing on to him your observations. He will respect you for the time and effort of pointing out things about his behavior and attitudes he's unaware of. And there is no one better qualified to do that than his mom and dad, who are committed to his ultimate happiness in life.

I warn you, however, that this personalized investment will require two exceedingly valuable ingredients: concentration and time. It is impossible to make correct observations without concentrating on your child at given moments each day—not all day, of course, but periodically each day. Perhaps a notebook would help you remember and sift out meaningful patterns in the child's conduct. And—as is always true of important projects—your schedule must allow the time for such a procedure.

It's really a question of priority, isn't it? Believe me, your child is "making himself known" every day. Whether or not you are paying the price of concentration and time is a different matter entirely. To put it another way, if you are "thick and tired" of living with a child you don't know, read on. If not, read this chapter again.

2
The Bents in Your Baby

A pediatrician I know once told me that raising children was somewhat like baking a cake—you don't realize you've got a disaster until it's too late! In certain cases, that may be true. However, if we are getting to know our children by patiently watching and listening to them, we can often detect that certain "disasters" are in the making. God will give sensitive parents a great deal of insight so disasters can usually be averted.

In the previous chapter, we looked into Prov. 22:6:

Train up a child in the way he should go,
Even when he is old he will not depart from it.

A paraphrase might read something like this: "Adapt the training of your child so that it is in keeping with his God-given characteristics and tendencies; when he comes to maturity, he will not depart from the training he has received."

We thought about how differently God has made all children and therefore how essential it is to remain keen and sensitive to their actions. By so doing we come to know them as individuals.

We concluded the chapter by admitting that such parental attention requires concentration and time . . . two very costly commodities in the twentieth century.

I find it refreshing, however, to see many parents willing to pay whatever price and sacrifice is necessary to see their children raised correctly. If you are among that growing number of conscientious parents, you long to know what to look for in your child. You need a handle to grab, some specific and objective things to be aware of.

To simplify my suggestions, let's think in terms of two major "bents" we should be aware of in our children. Remember now, these bents are built into your child . . . prescribed from birth. And these bents are found in *every* child regardless of race, color, location, religion, or economic status of their parents.

First, every child has bents or tendencies toward *good*. There are certain characteristics woven into the inner fabric of each child that give him his physical features, emotions, basic personality, interests, and abilities. We'll call these tendencies the "good bents" for lack of a better description. They are productive and beneficial to the child and the world he enters.

Second, every child has bents or tendencies toward *evil*. There are certain characteristics within every child that inevitably result in conflict, heartache, anxiety, and selfishness. This evil bent is inherited, originally from Adam and specifically from mom and dad. It is the sinful nature of humanity passed on from parent to child, from one generation to the next. An additional factor that cannot be ignored in this evil bent is a chain of sinful characteristics that can be traced back through each child's ancestors. That may seem confusing to you now, but as we allow the Scriptures to address these things, it will become clear.

Let's take them in order; first the good bent, then the evil.

THE GOOD BENT

As we have noted, the parent who is wise in the parent-child relationship constantly keeps in mind the tendencies God has built into his child. This is especially true as we discover and cultivate the things that are good and beneficial in each child's makeup.

Psalm 139 describes the "good bent" God gave to us—each one of us individually—before we were born. It's a remarkable passage.

Keep your child in mind as you read. If you have none, apply this to yourself. Think back to the prebirth period and consider what Ps. 139:13-16 is saying.

> For Thou didst form my inward parts; Thou didst weave me in my mother's womb. I will give thanks to Thee, for I am fearfully and wonderfully made; Wonderful are Thy works, And my soul knows it very well. My frame was not hidden from Thee, When I was made in secret, And skillfully wrought in the depths of the earth. Thine eyes have seen my unformed substance; And in Thy book they were all written, The days that were ordained for me, When as yet there was not one of them.

The *Thou* in this verse is highly emphatic in the Hebrew text. It means "You, God, and no other." Mother Nature didn't form me. Nor did I just happen. "You, God, and none other, were responsible for my formation." The word *form* means "originate." "For You, God, originated my inward parts." And *inward parts* is the term "kidney" in the Hebrew. It would include all the vital organs—the lungs, the kidneys, the liver, the brain, the heart—the parts of us that are life-giving and life-sustaining, without which we could not live. "You, God, originated within me those vital organs."

The psalmist goes on to say, "Thou didst weave me in my mother's womb." The Hebrew word *weave* means "to knit together in a mass or thicket"; it's the picture of the inner workings of the body. In that embryonic, fetal form, God weaves together each child as He wants it to be made.

In verse 14, David praises God for this thought. He says, "I will give thanks to Thee, for I am fearfully and wonderfully made."

But he doesn't stop there. "My frame [the word means "bony substance" or "skeleton"] was not hidden from Thee when I was made in secret, and skillfully wrought in the depths of the earth." How beautiful in the original text! *Skillfully wrought* is a picture of variegated colors, like tapestry or fine needlepoint. The same word is used in the book of Exodus when God describes the inner curtains for the tabernacle. They were to be made, fitted, formed, and embroidered together in special ways so the tapestry revealed a unique beauty.

A young man in our church is in his second year of medical school at the University of Southern California. He recently shared with me how this passage came to life in his mind as the students of his class were observing the internal anatomy of the human body. As he peered intently into the secret chambers beneath the skin, he saw the incredible network of organs (of various colors) surrounded by a myriad of veins and arteries. He commented that he thought about Psalm 139 and how beautifully David describes this truth.

Like fine needlepoint, God knitted us together "in secret . . . in the depths of the earth." This is an idiomatic phrase for a place of protection or concealment—a lovely, vivid description of a mother's womb. In that protected place, God oversaw my prebirth period as He fashioned and formed me like fine needlepoint.

Now look at verse 16. "Thine eyes have seen my unformed substance. . . . " *Unformed substance* are the words meaning "embryo." The word *seen* is literally "watched over." "God, You watched over, You oversaw my embryo as an architect would watch over a building under construction he has designed. You had in Your mind a plan, and You watched over that prenatal period so I was formed and fashioned just as You wanted me to be."

Let's go one step further. "And in Thy book they were all written, The days that were ordained for me." When you read that, you understand that God has, in our terms, a "book" for every child. You have three children; He had three books in mind. And He put into living form the plan of three books as He set them in your home. As each child was born, another book was opened. Different as night and day, but each one was planned and established, prescribed by God.

General Motors cars carry the emblem "Body by Fisher." You see that slogan every time you open the door of one of their cars. It's their trademark. Similarly, our bodies bear the mark of the Creator . . . "Body by God." That's right! The body, the frame you have—even the inner workings of your personality—were designed by God. And that is also true of your appearance, your emotional makeup, your areas of interest, your academic ability, and your artistic or athletic skills.

Now let's put it all together. This is what David is saying: "You, God, and none other, originated my vital organs. You knitted me together in the womb of my mother. My skeleton was not hidden from You when I was made in that concealed place of protection. When my veins and arteries and personality were skillfully embroidered in variegated colors like fine needlepoint, Your eyes watched over me when I was just an embryo. And in Your book, the days that I should experience were described— the days that would shape me into the person You want me to be."

Consider this carefully: The wise parent realizes the sovereign God of heaven has given the gift of children He has planned and arranged and prescribed with certain attributes, abilities, personalities, and physical appearances. By study and observation, this parent gets to know the child God has given him. He spends time in prayer, asking for wisdom. He spends time watching, talking with, and listening to that precious child, not just when he is little but all through the years the child is at home. The parent actually becomes a *student* of the child, because the parent knows this child has certain established bents. With keen discernment the observing parent takes special note of traits that begin to emerge. He studies the child in hopes of giving him wise, intelligent direction during those crucial growing-up years.

We had some friends in our home recently who were helping us work in the yard. One of them asked my wife, "How could you two have two girls so different?" He was right. (If he knew us better, he would ask, "How could you two have *four* so different?")

THE GOOD BENT APPLIED

It's remarkable! Same training, same parents, same environment, but each child is completely unique and distinct.

Now stop and think. Think about your own personality, the way God made you. As an adult you have come to see yourself more clearly . . . more accurately. Perhaps that self-discovery has been a painful one. It often is. Perhaps you did not get insights into your life from your parents. How much easier it would have been if you had!

Let's learn a lesson from all this. One of the best investments you can make is to deposit into your child's mind an understanding of himself—how he has been "bent." Help your child come to a realization of his God-given abilities and interests. Encourage him to accept himself and see the benefits and value of those traits that make him *him*.

Consider the alternative. As a child gets older, he may reason, "I am willing to be taught, but they don't understand what is inside me." Often, to bring about obedience, force is exhibited by a bigger person, dad or mom. Sheer force causes the child to rebel or run. He slowly develops disregard for those who are raising him. He resists and resents those who could help him understand himself but are unwilling to take the time.

You may say, "By forcing him I'm training him as the Bible says." No. Step one is not forcing but *knowing* your child. He is made a special way. No amount of forceful training will be successful if you fail to know your child.

This is a very real problem in homes where the father is trying to silence the frustrations of his own past through the life of his son. Consider the familiar scene of an athletic father who has an artistic son. The dad (who almost went into professional football but got injured in college) buys his boy a twenty-five-dollar football when the kid turns three! Day after day the father anticipates his son's love for football. But all the boy wants to do is play the piano.

By the time Junior is ten, Dad is about to lose his mind. He's got a kid who can play Paderewski's Minuet but can't catch a pitch-out. And to make matters worse, he isn't interested in learning! Dad yells louder. Son tries to explain. Dad refuses to listen and attempts to force a change by using public embarrassment as a lever or he threatens to stop the piano lessons. Son wants to please, but no matter how hard he tries he just can't get the coordination together. Dad and Son develop the amazing ability to live in the same house without speaking. They ride in the same car (to church!) and except for occasional grunts and glances, you'd think they were alone. Time passes. Football seasons come and go, bringing mute reminders of the conflict that remains unresolved.

Dad, a devout, church-going Christian, expects his son to be equally interested in the Lord. He's not. A curious yet common phenomenon occurs: a strange trade-off results in the relationship. Because of Dad's frustration and Son's resentment, a slow but steady erosion of interest in spiritual things transpires.

Change a few details and you can possibly read into this imaginary situation a similar scene that's painfully real in your own home today. How much better it is to spend your energy cultivating and encouraging the God-given qualities that will result in your child's reaching his maximum potential.

THE EVIL BENT

Two other passages from the Psalms describe the second bent. Your child has a general bent toward evil. Wise is the parent who sees this. If you fail to acknowledge the bent toward evil present in your child through inherited sin, you will fail to understand his battles, and your efforts will be a study in futility. You will simply scream louder and hit harder. And you won't be able to understand why your child is not cooperating.

Your child is bent toward evil because he is born spiritually dead. That may sound severe, but it is the truth. Psalm 51:5 states: "Behold, I was brought forth in iniquity, And in sin my mother conceived me."

At first glance, it would seem a mother is sinning when she conceives a child. Some would teach that the act of conception is wrong and sinful, but that's not what the psalmist is saying. I think the Amplified Bible puts it best: "Behold, I was brought forth in a state of iniquity. My mother was sinful who conceived me. And I, too, am sinful."

In other words, regardless of how dear and precious our mothers and dads may have been, they too had sinful natures. Aside from Jesus Christ, the unique virgin-born Son of God, every person who has ever drawn a breath has been born spiritually depraved and dead. No matter how beautiful and well-formed a newborn may be, the Scriptures declare he is, by nature, alienated from God. The psalmist is saying, "From the very start I was a transgressor. By nature, I was a sinner."

Psalm 58:3 expresses the same thought: "The wicked are estranged from the womb; These who speak lies go astray from birth." The wicked wander from the womb from the very beginning of life. Notice carefully: *from the womb—from birth.*

Hundreds of years later, the apostle Paul writes:

Therefore, just as through one man sin entered into the world, and death through sin, and so death spread to all men, because all sinned (Rom. 5:12).

Paul is simply verifying what King David wrote in the Psalms. From the beginning of life, every child is bent toward evil.

I was interested to read a statement from the Minnesota Crime Commission, a secular body presumably neutral on any spiritual issue. They were grappling with the rise in crime rate and attempted to come up with a reason for heightened statistics. The statement said in part:

Every baby starts life as a little savage. He is completely selfish and self-centered. He wants what he wants when he wants it—his bottle, his mother's attention, his playmate's toy, his uncle's watch. Deny these and he seethes with rage and aggressiveness, which would be murderous were he not so helpless. He is, in fact, dirty. He has no morals, no knowledge, no skills. This means that all children, not just certain children, are born delinquent. If permitted to continue in the self-centered world of his infancy, given free reign to his impulsive actions, to satisfy his wants, every child would grow up a criminal, a thief, a killer, a rapist.

The wicked *are* estranged from God!

Parent, if you think you can know and train your child correctly, yet all the while ignore the damage in his spiritual soul, you are sadly mistaken. You can love him with all your heart, more than life itself, but you must face the fact that he is marred and fallen because of sin. He needs restoration. He needs to be rightly related to God. The only way his problem of inherited sin can be handled is through counteraction, through a power greater than the power of depravity. The name of that power is the Lord Jesus Christ. In order for that counteraction to happen, the child must come to know Christ Jesus in a personal way—by faith.

A final passage regarding the general bent toward evil is Prov. 29:15. God's counsel is, "The rod and reproof give wisdom." When we deal in a later chapter with the subject of child discipline, we'll explain in greater detail the difference between the rod and reproof. But let me simply say there is more to correction and disciplining than the rod. That's part of it, but reproof is of tremendous importance in the rearing of a child. The rod *and* reproof give wisdom.

The other half of Prov. 29:15 states: "But a child who gets his own way brings shame to his mother." That is an unfortunate and misleading rendering. Literally, the passage says, "But a child *left* brings shame to his mother." Some editor must have felt it would be helpful for us to see that if a child gets his own way, he will bring his mother shame. That may be true, but the real thrust of it is that the child left *in the original condition in which he is born* will bring shame to his mother. Deposit a child into society, having fed him, clothed him, given him his desires, having done nothing to alter or counteract the bent toward evil, and he will shame you. He will bring increased havoc and heartache into a world already scarred by unchecked wickedness.

Counteraction through the power of Christ is a vital part of breaking the bent. You see, with the good bent, there has to be human cooperation. But with the evil bent, there must be divine counteraction. You can't ignore either if you wish to train your child correctly.

But wait. Some of you who read these pages have older children who know Jesus Christ, but they are giving you grief in specific realms of wrong. Perhaps it is rebellion or lying or profanity or gross immorality or a deceitful life-style or a vicious temper. You are probably brokenhearted and confused. Your child came to know Christ, but you cannot tell it today.

Why not? Didn't the power of Christ counteract the child's sinful nature? Yes . . . generally speaking. Your child is a Christian, but there are specific evil bents he inherited from his parents . . . and grandparents . . . and (are you ready?) *great grandparents* which have not been curbed. Let me clarify that.

Go back with me to Ex. 20:4-6:

> You shall not make for yourself an idol, or any likeness of what is in heaven above or on the earth beneath or in the water under the earth. You shall not worship them or serve them; for I, the Lord your God, am a jealous God, visiting the iniquity of the fathers on the children, on the third and the fourth generations of those who hate Me, but showing lovingkindness to thousands, to those who love Me and keep My commandments.

This is a direct quotation from the Ten Commandments. It is the second commandment followed by a principle as timeless as it is true. It's the principle that interests us: God deals severely with disobedience. Being jealous for our love, He does not smile at wrong nor does He overlook it.

A similar passage occurs in Ex. 34:5-8:

> And the Lord descended in the cloud and stood there with him as he called upon the name of the Lord. Then the Lord passed by in front of him and proclaimed, "The Lord, the Lord God, compassionate and gracious, slow to anger, and abounding in lovingkindness and truth; who keeps lovingkindness for thousands, who forgives iniquity, transgression and sin; yet He will by no means leave the guilty unpunished, visiting the iniquity of fathers on the children and on the grandchildren to

the third and fourth generations." And Moses made haste to bow low toward the earth and worship.

Of specific interest to us is the last part of verse 7, " . . . visiting the iniquity of fathers on the children and on the grandchildren to the third and fourth generations." Interestingly enough, the Hebrew word *iniquity* in Ex. 34:7 is the word "to bend," "to twist," "to distort," "to pervert." Thus, the verse is saying: " . . . visiting the bents, the twisting distortions, the perversions of the fathers on to the children to the third and fourth generations."

Hold on. We'll be right back. I want you to know this word *iniquity* is the same Hebrew word rendered in another way in Prov. 12:8:

A man will be praised according to his insight,
But one of perverse mind [the very same word] will be despised.

It seems clear from Scripture that in the visiting of iniquity upon one generation after another, there is a sustained "strain of perversion." That is highly significant! Read that sentence again. What I am suggesting is that the same "strain of perversion" in a parent or grandparent will most likely appear in a descending child if it is not sufficiently curbed.

At first glance, this appears to be an awfully severe verse of Scripture. When I first began to study it, I thought, "How vengeful of God to do such a thing . . . how unfair!" And yet quite the opposite is true. He could have visited that same perversion, that distortion or bent, throughout the *entire* family history. Ultimately that would result in the very annihilation of mankind. But He says, "No, it will be visited until the third and fourth generations."

Notice in verses 6 and 7 that the context is God's kindness and compassion. "The Lord God, compassionate, gracious, slow to anger, and abounding in lovingkindness and truth. . . . " He keeps lovingkindness for thousands. He forgives iniquity and transgression and sin.

Why then does He say a bit later, "No, I will visit upon one father and then his son and then his grandson the iniquity of that father"?

The culprits here are those who do not deal with their bents.

That is when our God of love gets tough! God forgives sin, and He wants us to forsake sin. He will show lovingkindness, He will forgive iniquity, transgression, and sin when it's dealt with.

The Scriptures tell us:

He who conceals his transgressions will not prosper, But He who confesses and forsakes them will find compassion (Prov. 28:13).

If we confess our sins, He is faithful and righteous to forgive us our sins and to cleanse us from all unrighteousness (1 John 1:9).

How loving and gracious is God to give us the power to deal with sin as He expects it to be dealt with. But when sin is *not* dealt with, either in our own lives or in the lives of our children, we must pay the price. We become, in the terms of this verse, "guilty."

THE EVIL BENT APPLIED

My wife and I have four children. The youngest is an unbelievable carbon copy of his daddy . . . *me!* Cynthia tells me at times that she fully understands some of the struggles that my mother once lived with. She is right. I can hardly believe my eyes on certain occasions. He is an instant replay of the same specific bents that are living inside my own skin. Do I ever feel guilty!

My problem? These bents were not curbed in me. I was not trained to detect those evil strains I inherited from my parents. What haunts me is the thought that his wife one day will have to live with a husband who has many of the same tendencies as I. I can assure you, curbing those specific, parent-inherited bents is no easy task.

Tying together the Exodus 20 passage with this one in Exodus 34, we would say God promises to give constant grace, lovingkindness, and mercy when we walk in His light. When we hear and obey Him, He promises blessing. If we willfully refuse to deal with sin as it occurs in our lives or in the lives of our family, the punishment will be felt consistently in the family tree. Is this concept supported in Scripture? Indeed it is.

When the nation of Israel split into two kingdoms after civil war had broken out at the end of Solomon's life, Jeroboam became the leader of the Northern Kingdom; Solomon's son, Rehoboam, the leader of the Southern Kingdom. Jeroboam was the first wicked leader of the Northern Kingdom, which lasted over two hundred years. Even though the Israelites had prophets who preached and declared the truth of God, they walked against Him. Twenty-one times in the Old Testament books of Kings and Chronicles you read the words that the nation of Israel "walked in the sins of Jeroboam." In other words, his sons and his grandsons did the same things Jeroboam did. What an indictment! Those same bents Jeroboam had were passed down. Specifically, they were the bent of idolatry, the bent of rebellion, and the bent of sensual immorality. All three sins were rampant in the history of the Northern Kingdom.

But let's go back even earlier to perhaps the most famous family in all the Bible—the family through which the Jews became a nation—the family of Abraham. I want you to see that the bent of lying with which they were infected began in Abraham and was not checked. As a result, it was passed on to his son and was not dealt with there. Then it showed up in his grandson, and still was not corrected. The eventual outcome was massive deception by a "professional schemer" named Jacob. We will begin at Gen. 20:1-5a:

> Now Abraham journeyed from there toward the land of the Negev, and settled between Kadesh and Shur; then he sojourned in Gerar. And Abraham said of Sarah his wife, "She is my sister." So Abimelech king of Gerar sent and took Sarah. But God came to Abimelech in a dream of the night, and said to him, "Behold, you are a dead man because of the woman whom you have taken, for she is married." Now Abimelech had not come near her; and he said, "Lord, wilt Thou slay a nation, even though blameless? Did he not himself say to me, 'She is my sister'? And she herself said, 'He is my brother.' In the integrity of my heart and the innocence of my hands I have done this."

That was lie number one, because it implied the absolute falsehood that Sarah was only his sister; she was his half-sister, but Abraham was living with her as his wife. Some people think, "Well, after all, everybody has a tendency toward this every once in a while." But it's still a lie.

The world has gotten soft today, it seems, toward lying. We

just took two years out of our national history in an attempt to uncover the lies surrounding the 1972 election proceedings. There is still lingering doubt as to who told the truth. The newsprint about Watergate was barely dry before new questions arose about whether the secretary of a prominent congressman was paid to work from eight in the morning to five in the evening or from eight in the evening until five in the morning. There are still conflicting reports.

Listen, these matters do not begin in *society*; they begin in *people*. Individuals. But they spread from one person to a system just as they spread from one individual to a family. Our sins *will* find us out.

Abraham's lie regarding Sarah was no isolated event. Abraham had a habit of lying. This was a weakness in his character.

And it may be a weakness in your character. Abraham's story may speak volumes to you because you find yourself developing an ability to lie and not checking it. You may check your own memory, recalling that all through your childhood you lied and got away with it. You may also be ashamed and frightened to realize your children are becoming liars just like you. We are living in a social mentality in which those matters are called "white lies" when in actuality they are dirty to the core. And they are to be forsaken.

Abraham never did forsake his habit. We can go back to Gen. 12:10-13 and discover his consistent "lying" bent:

> Now there was a famine in the land; so Abram went down to Egypt to sojourn there, for the famine was severe in the land. And it came about when he came near Egypt, that he said to Sarai his wife, "See now, I know that you are a beautiful woman; and it will come about when the Egyptians see you, that they will say, 'This is his wife'; and they will kill me, but they will let you live. [Who is he looking out for? Number one. He's looking out for Abraham. "Now, Sarah, when we get over there to Egypt, they're going to spot that you're a good-looking woman, and after all, they are going to want to take you with them and leave me behind."] Please say that you are my sister so that it may go well with me because of you, and that I may live on account of you.

Just in passing, wives, let me point out that God dealt severely with Abraham, not with Sarah. Why? Because under his direction she did as he asked. And when divine retribution came, it came directly upon Abraham.

Look at Gen. 26:6,7 for the discouraging continuation of the story. The Genesis 26 account is a record of a day in the life of Isaac, Abraham and Sarah's son. As you read this account, you may find yourself saying, "It seems like I've read this somewhere before."

So Isaac lived in Gerar. When the men of the place asked about his wife, he said, "She is my sister," for he was afraid to say, "my wife," thinking "the men of the place might kill me on account of Rebekah, for she is beautiful."

Men, let's not think for a moment that our traits are not passed on to our kids—especially those traits which go unchecked, unconfessed, and uncurbed. Isaac said the very words his dad said, except he put Rebekah's name in place of Sarah's. But in Gen. 26:8, Isaac got caught.

And it came about, when he had been there a long time, that Abimelech king of the Philistines looked out through a window, and saw, and behold, [the King James Version says] Isaac was sporting with his wife Rebekah.

That doesn't mean they were riding bikes together, my friend. They were kissing and hugging each other. They were showing intimate affection. Abimelech looked out the window and saw Isaac putting the moves on his "sister." He said to himself, "This doesn't fit. You don't do that with your sister."

Then Abimelech called Isaac and said, "Behold, certainly she is your wife! How then did you say, 'She is my sister'?" And Isaac said to him, "Because I said, 'Lest I die on account of her.' " And Abimelech said, "What is this you have done to us? One of the people might easily have lain with your wife, and you would have brought guilt upon us." So Abimelech charged all the people, saying, "He who touches this man or his wife shall surely be put to death" (Gen. 26:9-11).

The very same bent that went unerased in the life of Abraham was picked up by Isaac. But the visitation of this twisted, distorted character trait did not stop with Isaac either. It went right on to Jacob. Take a look at Gen. 25:19-26 as we go to the next generation.

Now these are the records of the generations of Isaac, Abraham's son: Abraham became the father of Isaac; and Isaac was forty years old when he took Rebekah, the daughter of Bethuel the Syrian of Paddan-aram, the sister of Laban the Syrian, to be his wife. And Isaac prayed to the Lord on behalf of his wife, because she was barren; and the Lord answered him and Rebekah his wife conceived. But the children struggled together within her; and she said, "If it is so, why then am I this way?" So she went to inquire of the Lord. And the Lord said to her, "Two nations are in your womb; And two peoples shall be separated from your body; And one people shall be stronger than the other; and the older shall serve the younger." And when her days to be delivered were fulfilled, behold, there were twins in her womb. Now the first came forth red, all over like a hairy garment; and they named him Esau. And afterward his brother came forth with his hand holding on to Esau's heel, so his name was called Jacob . . . .

Now just a moment. You probably know *Jacob* means "supplanter," meaning "to overthrow by force or treachery or deception." They named Jacob "one who overthrows," because from his birth, there was that inborn tendency to try to outdo his brother. He had a nasty habit of deception. He handled it beautifully with the habit of lies he began to develop at an early age, thanks to the help of his mother (not just his father). Let's rejoin the text at Gen. 25:27-28:

When the boys grew up, Esau became a skillful hunter, a man of the field; but Jacob was a peaceful man, living in tents. Now Isaac loved Esau, because he had a taste for game; but Rebekah loved Jacob.

You notice problems already, such as the problem of comparison. You'll notice the children were loved on the basis of how they pleased their parents or how they possessed the same likes as their parents, still a common problem today. Rebekah fell in love with Jacob because he was like her. Isaac fell in love with Esau because he was like him. The problems begin.

Later on, Jacob was cooking some stew. It smelled great! Esau

came home, and Jacob chiseled him right out of his birthright
while he was so hungry he couldn't say no. I've been that hungry
before myself. I can appreciate Esau's problem.

But wait—that's not all. Genesis 27:1-6 says:

> Now it came about, when Isaac was old, and his eyes were
> too dim to see, that he called his older son Esau and said to him,
> "My son." And he said to him, "Here I am." And Isaac said,
> "Behold now, I am old and I do not know the day of my death.
> Now then, please take your gear, your quiver and your bow,
> and go out to the field and hunt game for me; and prepare a
> savory dish for me such as I love, and bring it to me that I may
> eat, so that my soul may bless you before I die." And Rebekah
> was listening while Isaac spoke to his son Esau. So when Esau
> went to the field to hunt the game to bring home, Rebekah said
> to her son Jacob, "Behold, I heard your father speak to your
> brother Esau . . . ."

And she goes on to describe what Isaac said. You remember
the story—he put animal skins on his hands so he appeared to be
hairy, and perhaps changed his voice so he sounded like Esau,
and he came into the presence of his nearly-blind father, and his
father said to him in verse 18: " . . . 'Here I am. Who are you, my
son?' And Jacob said to his father, 'I am Esau your first-
born . . . .' "

He's lying. He's actually lying to his dying dad! He has developed the same trait that began with Abraham and,
unchecked, passed on to Isaac, and unchecked, passed on to
Jacob. And it not only went unchecked with Jacob, it was further
developed by Isaac's wife, Rebekah (Jacob's mother). And matters went from bad to worse. Here's why.

Remember when Jacob reached old age—the same boy, except
he is now grown and has a family—remember what happened?
He had a son Joseph, the apple of his eye. Joseph's brothers, the
other sons of Jacob, hated him. You will recall they put him in a
pit and finally sold him into slavery, and he wound up in Egypt in
a slave camp. They stole his multicolored garment (Genesis 37),
killed an animal, and dipped the garment into its blood. Then
they brought the coat to Jacob.

What did they tell their father? *They lied to him.* They said,
"We found this; please examine it to see whether it is your son's

tunic or not." When Jacob identified it as belonging to Joseph, he was grieved, but they didn't say a word. By their silence they lied again.

A famine hit the land. Joseph, whom Jacob's sons had sold into slavery, was now prime minister of Egypt. Those same sons of Jacob (all except Benjamin) went down to Egypt to get grain. They didn't know they were dealing with Joseph, but Joseph knew who they were.

So he said to them, "Is this everyone?"

"Oh, no," they said. "There's another boy with our father back in camp," referring to Benjamin.

Back home a few weeks later they were all eating supper together. They had brought Jacob a small portion of grain, with the promise there would be more if Benjamin returned with the others.

Father Jacob said, "Go back to Egypt and let's have some more grain." Let's follow the story in Gen. 43:3-5:

> Judah spoke to him, however, saying, "The man solemnly warned us, 'You shall not see my face unless your brother is with you.' If you send our brother with us, we will go down and buy you food. But if you do not send him, we will not go down . . . ."

Listen to Jacob (called Israel): "Then Israel said, 'Why did you treat me so badly by telling the man whether you still had another brother' " (43:6)?

That old liar! "How could you guys do that to me? Why did you tell him you even had a brother?" We don't know how old Jacob is here, but he is old enough to have learned a lesson. But you can see his bent was *still* unchecked.

A FINAL SUMMARY

The person who has in his home a child of two or three has a child who not only has traits and characteristics that are good, God-given, but he has a child who is bent toward evil because of a fallen nature. To be able to handle that Adamic nature, the child must be born again.

This is, of course, the highest spiritual priority—leading your child to Christ. You realize, if you are a wise parent, that your

child has in his system certain polluted traits which are characteristic of you, of your dad, of your dad's dad—traits that were
not dealt with properly. What's a parent to do? How do we detect
which bents our children have?

Proverbs 20:11-12 is still the best answer: "It is by his deeds
that a lad [or lass] distinguishes himself if his conduct is pure and
right. The hearing ear and the seeing eye, The Lord has made
both of them."

And look at verse 13: "Do not love sleep, lest you become poor;
open your eyes, and you will be satisfied with food."

Your child reveals through his actions the kind of person he is.
You *must* open your eyes. I believe this is what Mary, the mother
of Jesus, was doing when it is written she "pondered all these
things in her heart." During His childhood she observed, she
listened, she watched. Soon, finding Jesus had no bent to evil,
everything God had told her began to fall into place.

What am I saying? I'm saying you will discover the characteristics of your child as you study your child, as you use the
hearing ear and the seeing eye. No parent ever trained up his
child in the way he should go without making an effort to *know*
that child.

Let me ask you—when is the last time you sat down alone with
your child? With no one else around. An "appointment" with him
just to talk, to listen, to observe.

This is, in my opinion, one of the great problems caused by
television coming into our homes. I'm not going to go on a
blistering tirade about it. But let me say it will consume your
time so that in the final analysis you will have drifted (or in the
words of Proverbs—slept) through the most important years of
your child's life. Television mesmerizes our minds. It preoccupies
us. It "thickens" our thought life.

But so does the newspaper. So does work. So do community
projects. So do good, healthy, necessary, nice, important activities and involvement with other families. Nothing wrong
with these per se. But something is terribly wrong when these
things take the place of time with your children. You will never
know your children if you do not spend time listening to and
observing them.

If you'd like some good entertainment this evening, watch
them at play. Listen to them in conversation. Some of it will

crack you up. They are so funny. Know why? Because they sound *just like you* when you were that age. You know that tendency some people have to "take over"? Watch a little one come along and try to run everything. You think, "My, they got that from their mother." You will observe other things you've never noticed before. Your mouth will drop open as you say, "I had not realized what a need was there."

What do you do? Project No. 1: Do everything in your power to lead your children to Jesus Christ. Everything! Project No. 2: Spend time in prayer, asking God for insight and wisdom to see the character of your children in depth. Project No. 3: Become a student of your children. Talk about your children with your husband or wife. Make that a common practice in the quietness of your bedroom or around the table when the kids are not there. Determine to know those bents and characteristics in your children. Project No. 4: Do all you can to be consistent in discipline, in love, in reaction. Attitudes in our homes are far more important than actions, but they are not as easily detected. Project No. 5: Maintain an open and loving communication with the whole family.

Just the other evening I sat down with one of the children and had a long visit—an hour and a half—discussing the things on that child's mind. I listened. I did not rebuke. I did not preach. I did not read verses of Scripture to correct. I listened. I observed. I watched.

This child laughed. This child wept. This daddy loved every minute of it.

I relived that delightful visit in my mind several weeks later when I heard a song that had been in the "Top 40" in America for nearly a year. It's entitled "The Cat's in the Cradle."

My child arrived just the other day
He came to the world in the usual way
But there were planes to catch
And bills to pay
He learned to walk while I was away
And he was talkin' 'fore I knew it
And as he grew he'd say,
"I'm gonna be like you, Dad;
You know, I'm gonna be like you."

And the cat's in the cradle
And the silver spoon
Little boy blue and the man in the moon
"When you comin' home, Dad?"
"I don't know when—but we'll get together *then*, Son;
You know, we'll have a good time *then*."

My son turned ten just the other day.
He said, "Thanks for the ball, Dad.
Come on, let's play.
Can you teach me to throw?"
I said, "Not today, I got a lot to do."
He said, "That's okay."
And he walked away, but his smile never dimmed
And said, "I'm gonna be like him—yeah—you know
I'm gonna be like him."

And the cat's in the cradle
And the silver spoon
Little boy blue and the man in the moon
"When you comin' home, Dad?"
"I don't know when—but we'll get together *then*, Son;
You know, we'll have a good time *then*."

Well, he came from college just the other day
So much like a man I just had to say,
"Son, I'm proud of you.
Can you sit for a while?"
He shook his head and he said with a smile,
"What I'd really like, Dad, is to borrow the car keys
See you later—can I have them, please?"

And the cat's in the cradle
And the silver spoon
Little boy blue and the man in the moon
"When you comin' home, Son?"
"I don't know when—but we'll get together *then*, Dad;
You know, we'll have a good time *then*."

I've long since retired and my son's moved away
I called him up just the other day
I said, "I'd like to see you if you don't mind."
He said, "I'd love to, Dad, if I can find the time,
You see, my new job's a hassle and the kids have the flu
But it's sure nice talkin' to you, Dad;
It's sure nice talkin' to you."

And as I hung up the phone, it occurred to me,
He'd grown up just like me—my son was just like me.

3

You Can't Have One Without the Other

Several summers ago, my wife and I felt we should begin a class in our home for young couples with small children. Our desire was to study family living, using the Bible as our guide. A number of the couples in our church wanted to dig into the Scriptures to discover what God says about the parent-child relationship and the husband-wife relationship, during both the early and later years of marriage. We developed a real loving involvement with these we studied with during those ten or eleven weeks. There were eight couples in all.

I remember one evening I was prompted to ask a searching question: How many of you could say the home you were raised in was a home of real love, where you were accepted for who you were, where the discipline was consistent, where you trusted your parents' affection, love, and interest in you?

Since most of the couples had been raised in Christian homes, I expected a larger response than I got. Two people out of sixteen raised their hands, one reluctantly.

That evening has haunted me ever since. I have been prompted at times to ask a whole congregation the same question, but I won't because it would be embarrassing to those with their hands down.

You know in your heart that *at first* your own home was a loving home. You also know whether *right now* your home is a home of love. Something is tragically wrong if our Christianity, so solid and consistent on Sunday, is not permeating our homes with love, real love, Monday through Saturday.

You cannot love someone you do not know. That's basic. You cannot love the unknown. The heart and center of the parent-child relationship is that the parents are engaged in the process of knowing the children God has given them.

And this is a growing process. It's a crescendo. As the child increases in age, you increase in knowledge. By the time your child has fully matured, you are at ease in your understanding of him. There are no longer any major areas that are hidden.

Psalms 127 and 128 form a beautiful time-sequence picture of the progressions of the home. The scene is a domestic mural. When we visit places like museums of historical sites, we often notice murals in which the artist has conveyed the passing of years. As we walk along and observe the painting, we pass year after year in the history of the artist's subject. So it is with these two psalms.

The first two verses of Psalm 127 portray the home in its early years. As a man and wife join together as one, they begin to adjust to each other's lives—they learn to love each other. More than this, they learn as a couple to love the Lord. Verses 3-5 indicate the expansion of the home with the presence of little children. Then in the first three verses of Psalm 128, we see training in the home. Children given by the Lord are reared according to what God has to say. The last three verses of Psalm 128 are the twilight years, those years in which we as grandparents, and perhaps great-grandparents, learn to enjoy with delight those children God gave us.

The theme of both these psalms is happiness in the home. You cannot have a happy, healthy, harmonious home if you do not have the presence of love. "You can't have one without the other," as the song puts it.

To begin with, in the first two verses of Psalm 127, we have the beginning days in the home. Note the twice-repeated phrase, "unless the Lord."

Unless the Lord builds the house, They labor in vain who build it; Unless the Lord guards the city, The watchman keeps awake in vain (v.1).

Solomon, the writer of this psalm—a Jew himself—writes it with Jewish lifestyle in mind. The home is compared to a city. It was not uncommon for an ancient city to be built by having its walls finished first to keep out the enemy. Then, the city would be dedicated to the Lord by the city fathers. In fact, a plaque was often made and placed at the gate of the city, and the date of construction would be given.

What is Solomon saying? He is saying, "Unless the city fathers depend completely upon Jehovah and not just the city wall, the enemy will not be kept out."

In the same way, unless the husband and wife of the home trust wholly in the Lord, all their labor is in vain. As a matter of fact, I believe more and more that the building of a real home starts during courtship. That's why, in all my premarital counseling with young couples, there is a question I invariably ask: "Is your courtship pure? Is your courtship, right now, honoring to the Lord?" I can hardly remember an occasion where impurity in the courtship did not bring a damaging scar into the marriage.

Do you know when the sex education of your children begins (or began)? During *your* courtship! The values you live out during your dating years will invariably influence how you want your children to conduct their courtship some twenty or thirty years later. And they'll know, too!

Remember when you were fifteen, and you'd ask your mother a pointed question? Did you know when she was evading you? Of course you did. And you could tell when Dad sidestepped an issue. Inevitably your kids and mine will ask, "How far should I go?" Or worse, "How far did *you* go?" Unless your record was clear, or unless you have straightened a bad situation out with God, they will sense the shadows and are likely to live in moral impurity themselves.

Because of God's grace, the blood of the Lord Jesus Christ cleanses us from *all* sin. Thank God that He forgives, and that in Christ we can begin anew and start all over fresh again.

I frequently ask those who are dating and seriously considering marriage, "Are you right now engaged in a compromising sexual relationship?" Because if they are, I give them the option of either turning from their sin or finding someone else to handle the ceremony.

Am I harsh? No, I'm corrective. I'm not in the business of marrying people. I'm committed, heart and soul, to the establishment of Christian homes. Such homes *must* have a Christ-centered foundation. He alone must build the home. It cannot be *built* in the Lord if it is not *begun* in a relationship honoring to Him. "Unless the Lord builds the home, they labor in vain who build it."

Is the Lord the center of your home? I don't mean do you have a little plaque on the dining room wall that says He is the unseen guest at every meal, though that may be important to you. I don't mean do you have a big family Bible sitting on the coffee table which you refer to at times. That's not what I'm saying. I'm saying, "Is He the *center* of your home?"

It is immaterial whether you are a bus driver, engineer, secretary, banker, or ditchdigger. Whether you are a gardener or an airline pilot or a stockbroker makes no difference. Unless the Lord builds the home, is sought and obeyed in decisions, is the One who guides in those friction moments, is the One whose counsel is followed during the tough times (we all go through them), you labor in vain.

Solomon adds further wisdom when he says in verse 2: "It is vain for you to rise up early, to retire late, to eat the bread of painful labors . . . ." Have you found that to be true?

Some people say, "Well, our home isn't what it should be, so we'll provide a nice built-in pool out back." There's nothing wrong with a pool, but there's everything wrong when it's designed to be a substitute for what's missing.

Others feel that by working longer hours they can provide more things to bring happiness to the home. Such a philosophy is nothing more than empty materialism. In the words of Solomon, we "eat the bread of painful labors" when we adopt that philosophy.

Verses 3-5 refer to God giving children. There are *four descriptive phrases* or characteristics of children set forth in this passage. Each one is worth noticing.

First of all He says, "Behold [which means "Let me have your attention." He's tapping us on the shoulder, saying, "Hey, pay attention!"] children are a gift of the Lord." The first word to remember is *gift*. The Hebrew word means "property" or "possession." In verb form, it suggests the idea of giving an assignment to someone. Children are God's property which He assigns to you!

All husbands and wives borrow their children. Our children are not our own. Our children belong to God. He has loaned them to us for a season. Most marriages contain these borrowed jewels. They are not ours to keep but to rear. They are not given to us to mold into our image. They are not given to us so that we can force them to fulfill our lives and thus, in some way, cancel our failures. They are not tools to be used, but souls to be loved.[4]

That concept gives us a whole new perspective on children. God doesn't waste children. Nor does he waste parents. Verse 3 says, "Children are the property of God which He has given." Then it goes on to say, "The fruit of the womb is a reward."

I want you to see how this ties in with love. You love the Lord Jesus with all your heart—verses 1 and 2. You put Him at the center of your life. So whatever He gives to you comes from His love. It's what I call a "domestic love transfer." You are entrusted with the title deed to His property when your child is born. God gives you the children He wants you to have because of His love. They are considered, in His sight, His *reward*, key word number two. Not the result of a mere biological process, not a financial tax deduction, not another chair at the dining room table, not an interruption in your work. Children are assigned by God, His property, delivered to you as a loving reward for you to carry on the process He began. Remember, He's been designing and building that child for nine months!

Now consider the passage which follows: "Like arrows in the hand of a warrior, So are the children of one's youth. How blessed is the man whose quiver is full of them . . . ."

I think it's interesting the Lord guided Solomon to use the analogy of the *arrow*, which is the third descriptive term. Archery is one of the most difficult sports to master. Do you believe me? Give it a whirl! You can have a target as big as a mattress and at fifty paces you are doing well to hit any part of it. Even a person who is very gifted athletically, who is skilled and coordinated, has a difficult time developing as an archer.

I talked with a professional archer a number of years ago. He told me something of what is involved in shooting that arrow. I assumed that if you pointed the arrow in the right direction and let go, (and pray a lot!) it would land on target. That wasn't true. It was very important *how* you let go—the amount of tension on the bow, the position of your arms and shoulders, the release, where you fixed your eyes in relation to the tip of the arrow. It's an exacting skill.

Into your quiver God has placed particularly designed,

prescribed arrows. They will, by the wise parent, be drawn out, examined, and understood. God gives wisdom so the launching of that arrow toward the target will be a direct, central hit. God gives His possession as a reward; once in our hands, we can become skilled in the way we dispatch His arrows to the target.

Let me add something here. Not everyone has the same size quiver! Don't listen to the world when it talks about the "quiver"—the size of the family. You listen to God. We have a lot of information coming at us today through the media that has a way of drowning out the voice of God. Listen carefully, and He will make clear to you what the size of your family should be.

When God gave us our first child, a son we named Curtis, I thought that was great. Just perfect. A boy (like me) with curly hair (like Cynthia) and full of energy. I just *knew* we would be a one-child-only family. It was my third year in seminary (twenty-one papers due that year) which encouraged my conviction to stop there.

Two years later our quiver expanded. A darling, petite little girl we named Charissa. "Perfect," I mused. "One boy, one girl, one complete family." I quietly hoped God agreed.

He didn't. About four years later our second daughter enlarged our quiver . . . Colleen. What an added delight! New dimensions of love exploded in all of us. She brought an excitement and bundles of energy like you can't imagine. I now was holding secret prayer meetings regarding our "full quiver."

God ignored my petitions and along came Chuck . . . whom I was tempted to name "Omega." Now that quiver of ours is really stretched! But I have to be honest; we could not be happier. Each individual arrow from God has brought unique blessings and depth into all our lives. I'm so grateful God determines quiver size.

God will make Himself extremely clear to you on this issue— and on all of life's issues—if you listen to Him. He is an expert in these matters. The major issue is that He remains the central focus of your home.

Don't be frustrated if you are without children. Don't be frustrated if you have seven or eight. Relax. Children are assigned by God. Whether naturally or by adoption into a godly home, He fits certain kinds of children with certain kinds of parents. His Lordship extends even to making your quiver full. Think of it this way: Happiness is a full quiver, no matter what the size.

Look at Ps. 128:1, and check out description number four—

How blessed [how happy] is everyone who fears the Lord, Who walks in His ways. When you shall eat of the fruit [results] of your hands, [where did you hold the arrows?] you will be happy and it will be well with you.

Then He gives a very lovely, domestic picture.

Your wife shall be like a fruitful vine . . . Your children like olive plants around your table.

Your children are given as (1) *gifts* of the Lord, (2) *rewards* of the Lord, (3) *arrows* for your quiver, and (4) *olive plants*. The Hebrew says, "Your children will be like transplanted olive branches or shoots or seedlings." Notice the word *transplanted*. You see, God had His property. In the infinite ages past, God prepared in His mind a little seedling. During the days of gestation, God designed that little seedling, putting together those shapes and sizes and that distinct personality. Even the facial features and tone of voice. At the end of that time, there is deposited into your hands the little transplanted olive shoot to take its place as an olive plant around your table.

Fathers, next time you look around the table and you see those little ones, remember they are little olive plants. Your wife is the fruitful vine. Part of God's message here is that there are differences in your children. Olives grow from trees, not from vines. But it's interesting that the wife is in the innermost part of the house, like a fruitful vine. And each of these little separate pots sitting around the table is an individual, transplanted branch. What a beautiful setting . . . how tender, how perfectly arranged!

Let me illustrate this. One of the unsung heros of our church is the custodian. His name is Manuel—we call him Manny. Manny is a faithful worker. We see the results of his labor all about us. I am especially attracted to Manny because he is able to make things grow, and I'm not.

One day Manny and I had a talk. I asked him, "What is your secret? How do you do it?"

He said, "Come here . . . you have to talk to the plants." I looked at this lovely azalea bush that was bursting with blossoms. He said, "I sing to that one."

Believe me, with a track record like mine, you'll try anything. Soon after that encounter, a friend gave us a little peach tree. I planted that tree in our back yard which was at that time barren. We put all that gunk you buy at the nursery into the hole and set the tree down in there, packed dirt around it, and watered it.

When my friends left, I looked around and listened to be sure none of the neighbors were out in their back yards. I've never told anyone this story, not even my wife, but I began to talk to this peach tree. Manny said you were supposed to have a love for plants, so I began to sing to this little tree. I sang hymns and choruses and folk songs. I even threw in a couple patriotic numbers. You know what? This last spring it was filled with blossoms! Just a little transplanted tree covered with beautiful pink blossoms.

But then I got busy; my priorities changed. I forgot to water the tree, much less talk or sing to it. And it died. The only thing in the whole yard that was growing, and it died!

The afternoon I yanked it out of the ground that verse came back to me, "They will be like 'little olive plants'."

I still don't know whether singing or talking to a plant affects it. Maybe water alone would have done the job. But if I was willing to do all I did for a few blossoms, how much more should I do for those tender transplants at home! And the tragedy of neglect . . . my yard may not even make it during the millennium if I'm still in charge there, but you can be sure I'll go down swinging for those little olive plants indoors to make it! I'll sing love songs to them till I'm hoarse and hope the table is a jungle in the process.

Having considered these four characteristic words for the relationship of children with parents, let me conclude this chapter with a brief discussion of four checkpoints for carrying out that relationship with your children.

In Matt. 18:1, the disciples are visiting with Jesus, and they ask the question: "Who then is greatest in the kingdom of heaven?"

He doesn't answer *who*; He answers *what*—the kind of person who will enter with a degree of greatness.

He called a child to Himself and stood him in their midst, and said, "Truly I say to you, unless you are converted and become like children, you shall not enter the kingdom of heaven" (v. 3).

What's He saying? Unless there is a heart change and there is total dependence upon the Father, you'll not enter the kingdom of heaven. You should be just like a little child, who relies upon his parents.

Then, with that child still standing there, He says, "Whoever then humbles himself as this child, he is the greatest in the kingdom of heaven. And whoever receives one such child in My name receives me" (vv. 4-5).

The word *receives* is the Greek word that means "welcome" or "accept." Those of us who have been given children are commanded by the Lord to receive, to welcome, those children with the Lord's name attached to them. But He doesn't stop there.

> But whoever causes one of these little ones who believe in Me to stumble, it is better for him that a heavy millstone be hung around his neck, and that he be drowned in the depth of the sea (v. 6).

It's better for him that a big stone, the kind turned by a donkey when grinding wheat into flour, be attached to his neck and he be dropped into the sea.

Let me share with you from my study of this passage of Scripture four demonstrations of love that must be present in the home to produce a love relationship. Without these, your child will not be assured of your love.

Number 1: *The way we listen to our children.* If we refuse to listen to our children, we become stumbling blocks to them. I have in mind not only listening to what the child says but to what the child does not say. Do we *really* listen?

You know, the tongue is like a little bucket and the heart is like a well. Solomon says,

A plan in the heart of a man is like deep water,
But a man of understanding draws it out (Prov. 20:5).

Splashing down into the little heart and breast of your children, you enter into deep water. The parent who is wise gives careful interest to the child's words, because through his words the child reveals his feelings. Sure, he may be bitter and may have to be dealt with. I'm not saying it's always the parent's problem. But I am saying, wise is the parent who learns to listen when the child speaks.

There are little cries which come out at times. As they get older, children's cries become louder. The wise parent heeds the voice of the child. If you don't listen to your child, you reveal your lack of interest, and worse, a lack of genuine love.

Number 2: *The way we talk to our children.* I am appalled, even embarrassed at times, at the way people talk to their children.

Seldom do you hear such things as, "Dear, this afternoon Mom is really edgy, and I appreciate your understanding. I'm very sorry." Or "Son, I promised you I would do that and I broke my promise. I'm wrong. Please forgive me." Or "Honey, this afternoon what I said in front of those people I know must have embarrassed you. I shouldn't have said it that way." Or just sharing, "Thank you very much. I really appreciate that."

I was with a family this week that was a joy to behold. We sat around on the floor with the kids and we talked. The oldest brother had come home from school for the weekend. In some families, when the older brother comes home, friction develops and people start asking, "When will he go back?" Not here. In fact, there was such a love relationship that when one person talked, all the rest quieted down and listened. When one spoke, the others were right with him—"Yeah, that's right."

I thought, "Glory be to God! Here's a family that's *thoughtful* in the way they talk with one another."

Parents, develop this ability! Believe me, this family didn't suddenly become thoughtful; it's the result of practice. Are we too busy for that? If so, our Christianity is a mockery. We must have courtesy in our homes.

A number of months ago, a fellow came to me who had been sitting on an emotional lid so long that if the steam had suddenly come out, I think he would have shot up twenty-five feet in the air. The issue was family problems.

I asked him, "Son, what kind of a relationship do you have with your parents?"

His face was set. A frown came across his forehead as he answered, "I hate my dad!"

As I listened, he began to tell one incident after another when his father had embarrassed him, broken promises to him, or put him down, rarely having time for him. Finally the young man looked at me with an icy gaze and said, "I live for the day when either I leave or he dies!" (In fact, he had even made an attempt once to kill his father.) The one phrase he repeated continually was, ". . . the way he talks to me." There was no respect.

Parents, just because kids are little people doesn't mean you have the right to fire away. If your children are small, get down on their level when you talk with them. Kneel down occasionally for your visits—even before discipline. How would you like to have a nine-foot-four-inch giant come to you with a club in his hand, saying with a deep voice, "That's the last time you're going to do that!"

Why do our children run from us? We don't know how to listen to them. We don't know how to talk with them.

Number 3: *The way we discipline our children*. Two extremes: We're either inconsistent with not enough faithful discipline or we are too severe. My heart breaks on both accounts. My dear wife and I wrestle with it just as you do. We're learning like you're learning. Let's not give up hope.

I pray daily that God will help me with consistency. What was wrong yesterday is wrong today. What's right today will be right tomorrow. If there is to be a change in standards, let's call a family council and talk about the change.

The other extreme is an overkill on discipline. I had a young man in my home a number of years ago who was a Bible scholar like you seldom meet. He knew the Book backward and forward, original languages and all. But he had no family relationship.

His boy—a little fellow about eight years old—misbehaved a bit that evening, so his father locked him in the family car for the rest of the evening. Know what? That father may be able to walk circles around us in the book of Revelation or Romans or Judges, but he doesn't command respect. "But if a man does not know how to manage his own household, how will he take care of the church of God" (1 Tim. 2:5)? Perhaps today that boy resents his father. There was no love in his discipline.

The way you *listen* to your child reveals either a lack or the presence of interest. The way you *talk* with your child shows a lack or the presence of courtesy. The way you *discipline* your child shows whether or not you have compassion and conviction.

I once heard Dr. James Dobson make the comment: "The basic problem I encounter in dealing with parents is the idea that abundant love makes discipline unnecessary." Don't ever believe you can so love your child that you'll never have to discipline him. That's not only untrue, it's unbiblical. In fact, Heb. 12:6 tells us, "For whom the Lord loves He disciplines, and He scourges every son whom He receives."

Number 4: *The way we develop our children.* The way you get involved and help your child meet his or her goals is terribly important. You might be saying, "Well, it looks to me like it all rests on the parents." As a matter of fact, it does! Children, you see, are responders. Parents are the pacesetters, the givers.

I came across a penetrating verse of Scripture that summer we met with those couples for Bible study. It appears in a rather unassuming section of the Bible—the last part of 2 Corinthians 12, in which Paul is discussing his real love for the Corinthian Christians. They were his "spiritual children," so to speak. In verse 14 he says:

I do not seek what is yours, but you; for children are not responsible to save up for their parents, but parents for their children.

He's not talking about saving money. He's talking about the investment of personal interest, the free-flowing expression of love, a deep and abiding commitment to the development of the child.

We are the givers . . . the ones who look out for the best interest of our olive branches, cultivating and nurturing and paying attention to their needs.

Show me a parent who knows his child, who is sensitive to God's handiwork in the cultivation of that child. Show me a parent who loves that child so much that he could not possibly let him misbehave. Show me a parent who loves him so much that he cannot possibly have enough time to invest in that child, and I'll show you a child that's happy and healthy. Love breeds happiness. You really cannot have happiness without love.

Dr. René Spitz, a physician in New York City, reported on a

test a number of years ago. The results have since been put into several medical and educational journals.[5] The test was made on children, half of whom lived in an absence of love. The children were confined in two different institutions and were studied simultaneously. Both institutions were adequate in all physical respects, including equivalent housing, food, and hygienical standards. The institutions differed in but one factor—the amount of loving affection provided.

The contrast in results was dramatic. In "Nursery" the children showed absolutely normal development, some above average, according to Dr. Spitz. But after only two years in "Foundling Home" where there was no show of love, the emotionally starved children were not able to speak, walk, or feed themselves. With one or two exceptions in a total of ninety-one children, those who survived were human wrecks. In the words of one who conducted the test, these children "behaved either in the manner of agitated or apathetic idiots."

The mortality rate was equally startling. During a period of five years, 239 children who had been institutionalized for one year or more were observed. In "Nursery" not one child was lost through death. In "Foundling Home" there was a 37 percent mortality rate.

In a real sense, we love or we perish.

4
Straight Talk
on Survival Training

I was raised in the South. Most of my childhood was spent in Houston, Texas. By the time I reached my teen years, that city was fast becoming the murder capital of America. The city officials wrestled with the issues that caused such conditions. They came to several conclusions, but the one that stood out in my mind had to do with juveniles—since that's what I was! They discovered that most of the crimes were being committed by fellas and gals younger than eighteen.

I remember the massive propaganda program that began to sweep the city. Billboards, newspapers, and radios shouted the same message to parents. Signs like "Control Your Kids" or "Parents: Take Time to Train" were all over Houston. As part of this campaign to deter juvenile crimes, the Houston Police Department came up with "Twelve Rules for Raising Delinquent Children."

1. Begin with infancy to give the child everything he wants. In this way he will grow up to believe the world owes him a living.

2. When he picks up bad words, laugh at him. This will make him think he's cute.

3. Never give him any spiritual training. Wait until he is twenty-one and then let him "decide for himself."

4. Avoid use of the word "wrong." It may develop a guilt complex. This will condition him to believe later, when he is arrested for stealing a car, that society is against him and he is being persecuted.

5. Pick up everything he leaves lying around. Do everything for him so that he will be experienced in throwing all responsibility on others.

6. Let him read any printed matter he can get his hands on.

Be careful that the silverware and drinking glasses are sterilized, but let his mind feast on garbage.

7. Quarrel frequently in the presence of your children. In this way they won't be so shocked when the home is broken up later.

8. Give a child all the spending money he wants. Never let him earn his own.

9. Satisfy his every craving for food, drink, and comfort. See that every sensual desire is gratified.

10. Take his part against neighbors, teachers, and policemen. They are all prejudiced against your child.

11. When he gets into real trouble, apologize for yourself by saying, "I never could do anything with him."

12. Prepare for a life of grief. You will be likely to have it.

Had Solomon been mayor of Houston back then, he would have promoted that campaign. I'm convinced he would have encouraged parents to believe and apply the words he wrote: "Train up a child in the way he should go, Even when he is old he will not depart from it" (Prov. 22:6).

It's so easy to look to the school or the church and expect them to obey Solomon's advice. But Solomon knew nothing of either when he wrote that proverb. He wrote it to parents. *We* are best equipped to train, not the teacher at school or the minister at church. The school and the church look to the home for support. I have come to realize that neither the church nor the school can resurrect what the home puts to death.

Unfortunately, the well-trained child is the exception rather than the rule in our society. This was underscored in my mind when I overheard a teacher explaining to her friend the reason she had decided to retire from teaching earlier than she had planned. Her comment went something like this:

The problem is really *fear*. The teachers are now afraid of the principals. The principals are afraid of the superintendents. The superintendents are afraid of the school boards. The boards are afraid of the parents. And the parents are afraid of the children. But the children? They're not afraid of anybody!

Admittedly, she probably overstated her case, but there is

enough truth in it to make any parent think. Of course, the problem is not new. It goes back to the very first family—and the first child who was more than a rebel. He was a murderer . . . a disobedient boy who was not trained correctly.

"Training up" our child, remember, suggests two things, according to the usage of the Hebrew word. It conveys the idea of taming something that is wild. And it also indicates developing a taste for something good and nourishing. When we train our children, we initiate techniques that bring about a submissive will. We also discover ways to develop our child's taste so that he delights in things that are wholesome and right. None of this is naturally known by a child. These are things parents need to inculcate during those growing-up years in the home. When this is done correctly, God promises that even when the child reaches maturity, that "indescribable age of independence," he won't turn away from the training he received.

Back in the Old Testament, there is a rich and relevant passage of Scripture that shoots straight regarding child training— Deuteronomy 6. To help make the verses fit into your life and home, you'll need to put yourself into the sandals of those who historically heard this information. They weren't a group of Gentiles sitting in pews in a church listening to a preacher. They were, instead, the people of Israel listening to Moses, the man responsible for their deliverance from bondage.

Where they were is extremely important. When Deuteronomy 6 was written, the Israelites were on the edge of Canaan, commonly called "The Promised Land." There were some things about this new land which weren't very promising. It wasn't a vacation spot for the family, believe me. Dwelling in this stretch of land were the Canaanites . . . a degenerate, debauched, godless people. I personally believe you can trace the roots of modern pornography right back to Canaan.

According to the Deuteronomy 6 record, the Israelites were just about to invade that land and claim it as their own. God promised them they could overthrow the Canaanites. Yet, He warned them about that wicked life style. If they got sucked into the system, they would soon become as morally degenerate as those foreign tribes. Moses, the deliverer, was instructing his people in the importance of standing alone, maintaining their distinctives.

Look at what Moses says in Deut. 6:4-7:

Hear, O Israel! The Lord is our God, the Lord is one! And you shall love the Lord your God with all your heart and with all your soul and with all your might. And these words, which I am commanding you today, shall be on your heart; and you shall teach them diligently to your sons and shall talk of them when you sit in your house and when you walk by the way and when you lie down and when you rise up.

If you examine his words carefully, you will find that Moses was talking essentially to parents. First and foremost was to be their own relationship with the living Lord. The parents were to love Him without reservation, without limitation. In their own hearts were to be the eternal principles of God's truth. They were to be totally sold out to their Lord.

I find it highly significant that the ones who were to train were themselves to be "right on" spiritually. It makes sense. Phonies don't make good coaches. That's why Moses said, "These words, which I am commanding you today, shall be on *your* heart" (6:6).

As soon as he made that clear, he turned to the subject of training their children. The people were instructed to *diligently* teach their offspring. No passive, half-hearted, dreamy approach would work in Canaan. A hard-core system had to be met with diligence.

In our area of Los Angeles, there is the Rosemead Graduate School of Psychology. An extension of the ministry of this Christian institution is an out-patient clinic staffed by Christian counselors. A number of months ago, I asked one of those counselors what particular problem or struggle seemed to be the most frequent. He answered rather quickly: the passive male.

Diligence and passivity cannot co-exist. Moses' words are timely today. Our training must be diligent. Passivity is an enemy. Dads—we are to be the pacesetters. Moms—with equal vigor, you are to carry out the game plan.

God's method of survival training has a lesson plan. Guideline number one is clearly set forth: *Training is to be diligently carried out.* In a world system that is aggressively committed to capturing your child's mind and heart, no half-hearted training in the home will be successful.

The second guideline is closely allied with the first: *Training must start within the parent.* Nothing can really happen *through* us until it has happened *to* us. Children will have greater respect for instruction if they witness a genuineness in the models of their moms and dads.

In Phil. 4:9, Paul illustrates this point vividly:

> The things you have learned and received and heard and seen in me, practice these things; and the God of peace shall be with you.

"You want an example?" asked Paul. "How about me?" The Philippian Christians didn't have to follow an imaginary model. The one who preached to them was a pattern of the same truth. Small wonder the church at Philippi was so healthy and happy!

All this speaks volumes to parents. The oil of parental example helps remove the friction commonly found in the training process. So, moms and dads, it starts with us. That's an essential guideline to follow.

Moses then addressed the issue of getting the truth embedded into the lives of children so they could survive the Canaan cross-cultural impact. He said:

> And you shall teach them diligently to your sons and shall talk of them when you sit in your house and when you walk by the way and when you lie down and when you rise up (Deut. 6:7).

The Hebrew text uses an interesting word translated "teach them diligently." It means "to whet, to sharpen." It conveys the idea of an object piercing through another object. Something that makes a penetrating stab into something else. Your training is to penetrate, to pierce deeply into your child so as to make him keen, sharp, discerning. We are to "sharpen" our children as we train them.

The third guideline in God's lesson plan for survival, therefore, is: *Training should prepare the child to think for himself.* Overprotective parents, as well as easily-threatened parents, are weak here. Insecure moms and dads have great difficulty inculcating solid, biblical principles in their children apart from a long list of dos and don'ts. In many a Christian home a child is told what he may and may not do—but is not trained to understand *why*. That method, quite frankly, is lethal. As soon as Junior gets out of the nest (actually before) he is a ready target for the enemy's darts. His defenses are weak because he has merely learned his parents' lists. Deep within, he lacks the rationale, the conviction necessary to stand alone against a powerful world system.

Please don't misunderstand. I am not saying there are no dos and don'ts. A person who stands for nothing will fall for anything. Every child must have a standard—specific rules to live by. But as that child grows older and questions the family regulations, open and unguarded discussions must transpire. By allowing that to happen the child learns to think through his convictions with mom and dad as his sounding board. In the words of Deut. 6:7, the child is being "sharpened." Rigid, unbending, super-dogmatic parents who refuse to discuss the whys with their older children in a calm, intelligent manner have substituted telling for training.

One of the several unwed mothers with whom we shared our home comes to my mind. She was raised in a home where both parents were Christians—but terribly rigid. She was told what her moral standard would be. She was threatened by her father if he ever caught her in a compromising situation. She knew the rules of her parents—they were reviewed weekly, usually with a Bible opened on the table and a great deal of volume in the father's voice. She was never to question or reason or discuss the rules. She was to obey.

She got pregnant before she turned twenty. Didn't she know the rules? Yes. Weren't her parents sincere? Yes. Wasn't she aware of her actions and responsible for her disobedience? Yes. The deeper question is this: Was she trained to handle the temptation of lust? No. She had been told, but she had not been prepared to think for herself. My wife and I observed that this girl had difficulty thinking through most any conflict. She was indecisive and lacked discernment. The problem? She had not been properly *trained* in the biblical sense of the word.

Dr. Kenneth Gangel, president of Miami Christian College, spoke one evening in our church in Fullerton. Afterwards we talked about college students. I remember his words as though he spoke them yesterday. After more than twelve years of teaching collegians, he had noticed that the ones who had the most difficulty adjusting to university life were those who got "the list" at home. However, those who were given the freedom to develop their thoughts in keeping with Scripture while they were grow-ing up at home were the ones who seemed to sail through with the least number of problems. There were exceptions, of course, but hardly enough to remember.

Moses leaves us with a fourth guideline regarding God's lesson plan: *Training is to flow out of the natural setting of the home.* Remember what He advised? The Israelites were to talk (not preach) about the principles for surviving Canaan when they sat around in their homes, as well as when they walked or went to bed or got up in the morning to start the day. No big deal. No religious lectures. Just sharing through the natural flow of life in the home. Training of children was to be like the Scottish people say, "Better felt than telt."

Don't you love that? Isn't it believable? Talk about a perfect setting for learning! The home. During any given week there are dozens of opportunities to communicate God's way. And it's all so natural, so real. It just flows. Questions and conflicts come to the surface that provide a marvelous base for training. Wise is the parent who stays alert and capitalizes on such opportunities.

Take mealtimes. That's such a neat time for training. The olive plants are right there . . . each one a different size and shape, but all involved in discussing and laughing and sharing (and even complaining on occasion). A captive audience. They are too hun-gry to leave. What a choice opportunity to communicate. Of course, you can waste your mealtimes with comments like "How come the beans have these little white things in them?" Or "What stinks in the chicken?" Or you can use it for training. We often put on a stack of our favorite records for background music. Some-time we sing our prayer . . . occasionally holding hands around the table. After that I may share some event or some way God worked in my day. That often triggers the rest of our gang—and off we go.

Mealtimes are good times for character training. Many years ago Cynthia and I decided we all needed to work on our table manners. We were beginning to look and sound more like a pen of pigs than a home of humans.

Before supper began I whispered to Curtis (who was six) that he should serve Charissa (she was four) before he served himself. Naturally, he wondered why, since the platter of chicken sat directly in front of him . . . and he was as hungry as a lion. I explained it is polite for fellas to serve girls before they serve themselves. The rule sounded weird, but he was willing . . . as long as she didn't take too long.

Well, you'd never believe what occurred. After prayer, he picked up the huge platter, held it for his sister, and asked which piece of chicken she wanted.

She relished all that attention. Being quite young, however, she had no idea which piece was which. So, very seriously, she replied, "I'd like the foot."

He glanced in my direction, frowned as the hunger pains shot through his stomach, then looked back at her and said, "Uh . . . Charissa, Mother doesn't cook the foot!"

To which she replied, "Where is it?"

With increased anxiety he answered (a bit louder), "I don't know! The foot is somewhere else, not on this platter. Look, choose a piece. Hurry up."

She studied the platter and said, "Okay, just give me the hand."

By now their mother and father were biting their lips to restrain from laughing out loud. We would have intervened, but decided instead to let them work it out alone. That's part of the training process.

"A chicken doesn't have a hand, it has a wing, Charissa."

"I hate the wing, Curtis . . . . Oh, go ahead and give me the head."

By then I was headed for the bathroom. I couldn't hold my laughter any longer. Curt was totally beside himself. His sister was totally frustrated, not being able to get the piece she wanted.

Realizing his irritation with her and the absence of a foot or hand or head, she finally said in an exasperated tone, "Oh, all right! I'll take the belly button!"

That did it. He reached in, grabbed a piece, and said, "That's the best I can do!"

He gave her the breast, which was about as close to the belly button as he could get.

As the children talk, Cynthia and I listen. We listen to what is said as well as to what is *not* said. We stay sensitive to hidden attitudes that can't stay buried very long behind words. What are we doing? We are feeling the hidden edges of our children's souls. We are enjoying them and at the same time studying them. We are allowing the Lord to give us needed information which we may later be able to use in a one-on-one situation.

That is just one way we implement the truth of this fourth guideline. There are hundreds of other ways you can apply this principle of training. Food and talk flow easily together . . . so why not let 'er rip?

One warning, by the way. There is a thief in most every home. It has one big eye and it talks all day if you let it. It wants your attention and, if allowed to do so, it will get it. Strange thing about this thief. It's so selfish it won't let you get a word in edgewise. Families who let it have its way without any measure of control become hypnotized as it takes charge of the home. The thief, you know by now, is the television set. It's so easy to let it run on and on.

I'm an avid football fan. So is my older son, Curt. One weekend he and I were glued to one game after another. We grunted and groaned with each play as life went on unnoticed around us. My wife started to vacuum the carpet in the den, of all places, right in the middle of a very important series of downs. I couldn't believe it! I yelled above the noise of the game mixed with the roar of the vacuum cleaner, "What in the world are you doing, Cynthia?"

Her answer was classic. "I'm cleaning the stadium, Charles!"

Stab, stab. Twist, twist. I'll never forget it. I got a liberal arts education that day as God used her comment to awaken me to just how selfish we can become when the television controls us.

Let me suggest a family night at least once a week. (With no television, okay?) Plan ahead now. Perhaps your first night could be a brainstorming session where you gather suggestions of what to do on future family nights. Then do your best to follow through. The kids will grow to *love* it, believe me. And God will give you all kinds of insight into each child during these special evenings together.

Mix them up, now. Add variety and stay flexible. Table games are fun. So are trips to special places. How about long walks? Or a camping weekend? It's remarkable how a tent and a few cots plus an open fire and the smell of the outdoors will draw members of a family together like magnets. And in that very natural setting,

barriers are broken down as God communicates great chunks of
truth through looks and laughs and hugs and kisses. Wow! Makes
me all excited just to imagine that setting.

Now let's think about " . . . when you lie down and when you
rise up." Bedtime is an ideal time for training. Frequently I crawl
into bed with one of our children. I don't look over at them and
say, "Talk!" I just lie there and invariably my kiddo will snuggle
up as we both look up at the ceiling. It's dark and quiet. Life has a
way of getting pretty simple at night. Before very long those
little feelings will start to emerge. I listen. Talk about building a
relationship! Before long we're discussing something very important to that child. Therefore, it's important to me.

Before I get through with one, the others are saying, "Hey,
Daddy, my turn!" As I move into another room the same thing
happens again. Instead of bedtime being the hour of destruction,
it has become for us one of the most significant times of training
in the entire day.

The other evening one of our four was troubled. He was
obviously wrestling with a deep problem. I didn't know what it
was and I had to leave that evening. My wife, sensing the
struggle, said to me as I left, "You know, Honey, I'm going to go
in there and just listen to him." (I loved the way she said that.
Not, "I'm going to go straighten him out," nor "He'll get over it.")
Cynthia spent about forty-five of the most valuable minutes of
her entire week listening. Just listening.

The next morning the light had returned to his face. She said
something to me I'll never forget. "You know, I don't ever want
our children going to bed troubled. Things get locked in permanently when they lie down troubled. When they get up in the
morning it seems like the concrete is cured and hard—and it
takes days to break through the layer."

" . . . when you lie down and when you rise up."

Some of you have larks in your home. You probably have owls
as well. The larks spring out of bed early and wide awake. The
owls have trouble achieving blanket victory. They feel their way
along. In our home, we call them "springers" and "feelers."

I'm married to a "feeler." She married a "springer." (That's
often the case.) I bounce up in the morning and within a matter of
seconds, the old brain is clicking and I'm ready to talk or sing or
discuss the deepest subject imaginable.

Now that can irritate "feelers." They need time . . . and quietness . . . and tenderness. "Springers" are short on all those areas, unfortunately. Larks aggravate owls by trying to force conversation and saying things loudly. Owls tend to glare glassy-eyed and say things that are absolutely hilarious—but you'd better not laugh out loud.

It's really fun living with someone who is very different . . . but who also is such a complement and balance to my life. I thank God daily for the one He chose for me to team up with throughout life. How valuable she is to me personally and to our family!

We have learned that springer-feeler couples have springer-feeler kids. And it is terribly important that we realize we train our children as they "rise up" each day. Those who rise slowly must be treated with respect and gentleness. If there is a deadline to meet, an understanding but firm assistance will help. Those who bounce out early, full of enormous energy, need to be trained to be thoughtful of others. As the child grows older, it helps to have certain projects he can turn to soon after arising.

Years ago someone passed on to me a good way to begin each day. I employ it often and encourage our children to do the same. Three particular actions help us get in tune with God.

First—for the sake of the body, stretch. Stand up or sit beside the bed and give yourself a big stretch. That gets the inner juices flowing and starts the motor.

Second—for the sake of the soul, smile. Even if it is a slight, faint smile, do it. That sets the mind on a positive note for the day.

Third—for the sake of your spirit, say to yourself, "God loves me today!" Immediately, your focus is vertical rather than horizontal. The very first word of your day has been "God." If you are awake enough to do so, tell Him it's His day—not yours. Immediately make yourself available to Him and acknowledge His right to take full control of everything that happens in the hours before you.

Moses has left us a rich legacy. Even though we are thousands of years removed from his day, the guidelines are amazingly up to date. They are not only true, they will help our children survive when we are not around to shield them from the wintry blast of this cold world. Let's personalize the principles by reviewing them in the form of four questions:

1. Are you carrying out the training of your children in a diligent manner?

2. Since training must start within the parent, are you making a consistent effort to practice what you preach?

3. Is your training program preparing your child to think for himself?

4. Does the training flow out of the natural setting of your home?

When Solomon wrote "Train up your child . . . ," he said a mouthful, didn't he? The sobering truth is this: We *are* training our children whether we plan it formally or not. We are training them by the way we live.

Look over the shoulder of a wise father and read this note he actually wrote to his son Jeff late one night:

Dear Son,

Last night I came home late, sometime after midnight. As I have done many times before, I walked slowly into your room to kiss you good night, even though you had been asleep for several hours. At moments like this I look at you and think about the eleven years that we've shared together. They have been good years and I think back on them with warmth and happiness. There's a love between us, son, that is built on a mutual respect which calls forth obedience and kindness into a happy bond of camaraderie. Oh, I know you really don't know what that word means, but it really doesn't make any difference because I'm not talking about things now that you can understand. Perhaps they are even things that I do not understand.

You see, I'm looking beyond this day. A few years beyond. To the time when you will be a "teenager"—those so-called critical and turbulent years which misunderstanding adults have mistakenly made into a narrow valley of traumatic experiences through which a child must pass before he can become a man.

You know what some are saying, son? Psychologists educators, clergymen, all alike. They are telling us that we won't be able to speak to each other, or at least not understand each other, in just a few more years. Oh, you'll probably reside here in the house, and we'll have meals together and see each other occasionally, but we're supposed to live in two different worlds. They call it a "generation gap."

. . . .

It's really all based on philosophical relativism. That means that people think nothing is sure from year to year or even from day to day. They think that everything has to be questioned and expect that the questioning will probably result in change. This whole philosophy basically assumes that things are bad just because they're old and, I suppose, consequently that things are good just because they're new. It's the disease of presentism.

But you haven't been taught this way, son. You've been taught that there are absolutes, things which are fixed for all eternity by the determination of God. You have learned that there are certain standards which are set, not by society, but which come from a code far beyond the shifting views of man. You've been taught that love, obedience, faith, and honesty are virtues in any age and in any situation. If you believe what you've been taught, and try to live this way, you will be subjected to criticism and scoffing by the society in which you live. May God give you the courage to face it!

Well, maybe now you can begin to see why I wonder what lies ahead for us, young friend. Five years from now, will we still take bike rides together and talk about things that we're both interested in? Will we still sit on the living room floor and listen to Beethoven on one record and the Kingston Trio on the next and enjoy them both together? Will we go to church together and believe that what the pastor says is true because he's preaching about truths that are timeless? Oh, I know you'll think dad is square because he won't wear some of the clothes that happen to be in fashion for young men. You might not even like some of the rules that we will still have to maintain as long as you're living at our house. But will these little differences actually drive a wedge between us that can be called a "generation gap"?

I know if you were awake right now you would put your arms around my neck and tell me, "No, dad. Nothing can come between us like that. We'll always be together just as we are now." And I'd like to hear you say it, and I'd like to believe it. But we will really have to wait those several years to find out the answer to my questions here by your bedside tonight. Good night, son. I hope the future allows us to build a bridge across the gap.[6]

5

The Home Training of Jesus

Let's take a brief change of pace. Our attention has been exclusively upon our own homes and the importance of knowing and training our own children. It might help to get a glimpse of the childhood and growing-up years of Jesus of Nazareth. Most of us have seldom pictured what His life must have been like, partly because very little is known about it.

Dr. Luke records for us just about all we know of Jesus' early childhood and teen-age years which He spent in the home of Mary and Joseph. Most New Testament scholars think Joseph died before Christ actually became an adult, because Joseph is never mentioned as being alive during the ministry of Christ. It is possible, however, that Joseph lived through Jesus' teen-age years and had the privilege of watching Him grow toward manhood.

Now I know it is hard for us to think of Christ either as an active little boy or as a teenager. Yet it is stretching to consider what it must have been like to raise a child without a sin nature. We will never know that experience, but Mary and Joseph knew it in every sense of the word. They never knew what it was to have a disobedient boy.

Obviously, as we turn to a few verses in the second chapter of Luke, we're looking at a very unique situation, a very unique boy. Then, too, this young man lived at home for thirty years before He began what we would call His career. It's a little unusual for anyone in our day to live thirty years under his parents' roof, all things considered. In spite of the fact that He had no sin nature and that He lived that long at home, I still think there are some very appropriate applications of His life to our own homes today.

Look at Luke 2:39-40:

And when they had performed everything according to the

Law of the Lord, they returned to Galilee, to their own city of
Nazareth. And the Child continued to grow and become
strong, increasing in wisdom; and the grace of God was upon
Him.

In these two verses we are told of Jesus' life between infancy
and age twelve. In all of literature, that's all we know for sure of
His childhood. Then beginning at verse 41 to the end of the
chapter, we're told something of his life from age twelve to
thirty. Honestly, that's all we have. To use an old southern
expression, the Scriptures "go begging" when we look for any
further information about the childhood, teenaged, and young
manhood years of Jesus.

Verse 39 mentions that Mary and Joseph performed everything according to the "Law of the Lord" during those early days
of Jesus' infancy. This is important because it declares that Mary
and Joseph were meticulous about how they raised their Son.
They fulfilled every necessary requirement in the beginning
days and months of His life.

Then verse 40 tells us He continued to grow and become
strong. He grew in wisdom. "The grace of God was upon Him,"
we read. And that's actually all the Bible tells us about His
pre-teen years. But there's a lot we can draw from these two
verses.

When Dr. Luke tells us the child continued to grow and become strong, he's referring to Jesus' physical life. The way this is
written conveys a very normal, natural growth process. Please
keep in mind that Mary and Joseph realized they had on their
hands the Son of God, the promised Messiah, the Redeemer.
They had in their home one who was destined to become the
greatest individual the world would ever see. Yet, I'm impressed
with what it says about His physical growth—He continued to
grow and become strong. There's no force there. No parental
push. Mary and Joseph weren't antsy to get Him before the
public. He was obviously a gifted young man. And yet during His
days as a lad he was allowed to develop at a normal pace.

God may have given you a gifted child. That child might be
quite talented, and you're already noticing those talents. There
is a tendency among many parents to push a child like that; this
can create problems. The child is as unimpressed as he can be

while his parents are intensely exercised to get that gift under-
way. They are anxious for others to know what a beautiful or
intelligent or talented child they have. It's all part of getting
caught in the syndrome of our society. Our world pays heavy
tribute to such children. If we're not careful, we get caught in the
trap of having to prove what a superb creature we have brought
into the world.

If you have a gifted child, that's fine. It's remarkable how the
gift will take care of itself. It will develop. With parental encouragement, it's amazing how naturally your child will get it together. Jesus was given every opportunity to grow and become
strong. Written between the lines is a normal process of calm,
consistent development. I'll say more about gifted children in
Chapter 9.

Then Scripture says He continued to increase in wisdom.
Literally, Luke writes: "He continued to be filled with wisdom."
It's the idea of being filled up. A process is involved. It's the
Greek tense that conveys continued action. Just as he continued
to grow and become physically strong, so He continued to become filled with wisdom. The first part of the verse mentions His
physical life. This part of the verse talks about His mental perception. Perhaps it would be safe to assume it includes His
emotional life. He became, at that young age, filled with
wisdom.

I came across an interesting chapter in the New Testament this
week. It is 2 Timothy 3. Writing from a dungeon, the aged apostle
Paul addresses his close friend Timothy, a young pastor who
meant more to Paul than anyone at that time. He mentions in
verse 13 the conditions of the world in which they lived: " . . . evil
men and imposters will proceed from bad to worse, deceiving and
being deceived." In effect Paul is saying, "Timothy, that's the
kind of society we live in. You are ministering in a world of
deception. Some are deceivers and others are deceived." He is
encouraging Timothy to be alert to the evils of the day.

How can one be alert? Verses 14 and 15 answer that question.
As you read, notice the step-by-step process.

You, however, continue in the things you have learned and
become convinced of, knowing from whom you have learned
them; and that from childhood you have known the sacred

writings which are able to give you the wisdom that leads to salvation through faith which is in Christ Jesus.

Two things attract my attention. First, the importance of his childhood training. As Timothy faced the world of deceivers and those being deceived, he had to rest on the absolutes he learned as a child. When Paul writes, ". . . knowing from whom you have learned them," he is referring to Timothy's home, the people he knew as a child.

In 2 Tim. 1:5 we are given a glimpse of Timothy's home as Paul writes: "I am mindful of the sincere faith within you, which first dwelt in your grandmother Lois, and your mother Eunice. . . . "

What a heritage! His grandmother was a godly woman, his mother was a godly woman, and both passed on the same traits to Timothy. His godly home prepared him for living in an ungodly world.

The second thing that attracts my attention is the process that brought Timothy to his present frame of mind. Go back to 2 Tim. 3:14. Timothy first received knowledge. His mother gave him facts, reliable information, called in Scripture "knowledge." The second stage was learning. Knowledge was given and then he began to appropriate or learn those facts provided by his parents. Knowledge and learning then led to personal conviction. He became convinced of these things.

The same process occurs today. The facts and principles of Scripture are heard and understood by our children. That leads to learning. Then learning leads to conviction.

Finally, there is wisdom. Verse 15: " . . . from childhood you have known the sacred writings which are able to give you the wisdom . . . . "

Parents convey knowledge. Timothy's parents did. Jesus' parents did. Perhaps your parents did. Then from that knowledge you became convinced of certain things. Following this process there came wisdom. Wisdom is simply looking at life from God's point of view. It is the ability to apply biblical principles to everyday life. Wisdom is occurring when you glean from the Bible principles for living and then *apply them* to your life.

The president of a leading evangelical seminary of our day once said as he stood before the graduating class, "I am concerned that we are turning out men with too many beliefs and not enough convictions." The same could be said of our homes. Too many beliefs float around without practical roots. There is too little conviction.

So Jesus increased in wisdom, according to Luke 2:40. Then we read "the grace of God was upon Him." That's his spiritual life. If I may divide His life into segments for the purpose of clarification, we have His *physical* life. He grew and became strong. His parents didn't push him. His was a normal childhood. He also increased in wisdom. That describes His *mental* and *emotional* life. Although young, wisdom began to evidence itself. As these forces took effect, His *spiritual* life developed—the grace of God fell upon Him.

Are your children old enough yet for you to realize how the grace of God has come upon them? Isn't it a delight to witness God's grace in your children?

I will never forget one of the last conversations I had with my mother. She was standing over a sink. That is my most vivid memory of her—spending time doing the dishes after a meal. I looked on the wall in front of her where she had a small card, yellowed with age. It was a Scripture quotation from Prov. 18:16. It read: "A man's gift makes room for him, And brings him before great men."

I said, "Mother, why do you have that verse up there?"

I was intrigued by it, frankly. I hadn't really taken the time to meditate on what the verse was saying.

"Oh," she said with a smile, "I'm claiming that for all three of you children."

She was asking God to develop that truth in my older brother's life . . . my sister's life . . . and my life. She was asking that the grace of God might fall upon us, causing us to be used in others' lives. When God does that He moves in like a snow shovel, pushing aside whatever stands in the way of a gift. He makes room for it.

It doesn't take a parent to force it. Nor does it take a great deal of human ingenuity or brilliance. You simply entrust your children to the Lord. You come to know them and adapt your training accordingly. You pray specifically for God to use them . . . then watch out! God will make room for their gift. That's grace.

Let's turn from Jesus' childhood to a few years later. In Luke 2:51-52 we see His years as a teenager and young man. Aside from the incident in the temple (mentioned between verses 41 and 50), we know nothing more of His early years. Dr. Luke writes this about Jesus in His home as a teenager and a young man:

And He went down with them, and came to Nazareth; and He continued in subjection to them; and His mother treasured all these things in her heart" (v. 51).

He and Mary and Joseph moved to Nazareth. During those years, He obeyed them. We read that His mother treasured all these things in her heart.

I am captivated by the words . . . "He continued in subjection to them." You say, "Well, He was perfect. Naturally, He'd be in subjection." Yes, but there's more. He was perfect, but Mary and Joseph weren't. It's interesting—God the Father put the perfect Son of God in the home of imperfect parents. The Greek word translated *subjection* is a military term which means to "fall in rank under the authority of another." From a human point of view they were of higher rank than He during those formative years. Jesus was pleased to fall in rank under their authority.

In this book I have been writing mainly to parents. I'd like to pause and address you who are living under the roof of Mom and Dad, the children and young people who may be reading these pages. Are you really living in subjection to your parents? Do you fall in rank under their authority? Chances are, you are thinking, "Oh, yeah, sure."

Great! Let's see if you really mean what you say. Here are four questions I'd like you to answer.

1. Do you cooperate with their desires without griping? When they request something of you, do you do it without a complaint? A positive response is part of being in subjection.

2. Do you happily give up your rights when there is a conflict in the schedule rather than ask them to give up theirs? Are you quick to adapt and adjust with a pleasant spirit? Unselfishness is part of being in subjection.

3. Do you respond to their counsel and correction with appreciation? I'm smiling right now. I want you to think about

this one. Even if your parents aren't Christians, you are to obey. They care very little whether you can quote an entire book of the Bible to them. Remaining open to their counsel is part of being in subjection.

4. Do you fulfill your responsibility with a good attitude? Are you thorough and prompt as well? How does your room look today, for example? Are the dishes they asked you to do still in the sink? Still on the table? You see, Christianity gets gutsy at times. Your attitude is part of being in subjection.

A set of parents came to me a number of months ago. They admitted with a sigh that they could no longer deal with their daughter, who lived at home while attending college. She felt she had reached such spiritual maturity that only the Lord told her what to do. She had a verse of Scripture to counteract nearly everything they said to her. She was causing disharmony and disunity. Regardless of what they asked of her, she had a "biblical reason" for not doing it. They were at a loss to know how to handle a Bible-quoting, rebellious daughter. They had been fair and careful not to treat her like a little child, but she was taking advantage of her parents.

Remember, Jesus remained in subjection to Mary and Joseph throughout His days in that carpenter shop. There are few things more important to a parent than a submissive spirit in a child. Take it from a parent—it's true. It was Jesus' willingness to cooperate with His parents that Mary treasured in her heart. She never forgot it.

The last verse in Luke 2 reads: "And Jesus kept increasing in wisdom and stature, and in favor with God and men."

It sounds the same as His childhood, but it's different. The Greek word here translated *increasing* indicates more aggressive movement. It is a word of advancement, of definite procedure.

Jesus had come of age, if you please. As He worked as a laborer in Joseph's carpenter shop, He came to realize that within Him were unique abilities, obviously from God. Perhaps He began to realize there was a very serious calling ahead of Him. So He began to "move out," we would say. We don't find His parents restraining Him. He sensed this was His calling and began to advance toward a goal. He increased in wisdom and stature.

Parents, it is a normal thing during the early years for the emphasis to be upon the physical. That's why we read in those earlier verses that He increased in stature and in strength. But when your child comes to those teen years approaching manhood (or womanhood), it is a normal thing for you to see spiritual growth. Something is wrong if you don't. If your child of three or four prays in the evening, "Now I lay me down to sleep. I pray Thee, Lord, my soul to keep," that's normal. If he's still praying that when he's fifteen, there's something missing spiritually. Seriously.

I'll never forget one of the strongest rebukes my older brother gave me. When I was about fourteen years old, my mother asked me to lead in prayer at the supper table. At that time in my life I was indifferent to spiritual things. My brother—who was three years older—was not. So I prayed the same old bromide—"Lord, bless this food and make our bodies strong and free that we may use our health and strength in service for Thee. Amen."

As I reached for the potatoes after that momentous repetition, my brother looked through me and asked, "When are you going to learn to *pray*?"

He cut right to the heart of my indifference. I was still racing through meaningless words. They meant nothing at all to me. My brother stopped me short; it was a never-to-be-forgotten rebuke. I was not advancing toward any meaningful goal. I was spiritually "out to lunch."

Jesus, as a teenager, was moving ahead in wisdom and stature. He was also balanced. He was developing "in favor with God and men." I *love* that phrase. It is important to maintain a balance in the training of our children. It's so easy to make super-spiritual "freaks" out of the children we raise. This happens when we think all there is to living is "spiritual life," meaning church and religious activities. This passage says Jesus was found in favor with men as well as God. May I amplify this?

Your child is gifted musically. Are you broadening that musical gift? Or must he play only hymns? Is your child gifted in public speaking? Are you acquainting him with the value of public speech and debate in the dramatic arts at school? Are you broadening him? Are you getting him in touch with what is going on so he will be in touch with this world? Your child may have an excellent mind, loving to read. I suggest you introduce him to the classics. Broaden his mind so he can come in touch with the world of literature. His days in college won't be just dealing with the Scriptures.

Seek balance in the rearing of your children. Not either-or . . . but both-and. A gifted child in a Christian home doesn't necessarily have to become a preacher. The crying need in our day is for nonprofessional Christians—men and women in every level of life who can accomplish the very highest quality of work in their particular realms. It is unbalanced to teach our children that the only real career that matters is the ministry.

Jesus was raised in a balanced setting. He became a wise, competent carpenter before He ever began to teach and preach. His home training is a perfect model to follow. He was an individual who grew up in favor with God and men.

I spoke at a family camp in northern California two summers ago. The entire week was spent emphasizing the importance of God's hand in every calling, in every profession. We encouraged each Christian to realize that his or her vocation was ordained of God. It was their "ministry."

By the end of the week the message came through. One man shared how much the week had meant to him and his family. The director of the camp asked him what he did for a living. His answer was unforgettable. "What's my work? I'm an ordained plumber!"

Before Jesus was a teacher of God's truth, He was an ordained carpenter. That's balance. That was the result of right training. That's the kind of Christianity that's attractive and winsome to others.

Is your home training doing that?

6
Dealing with Rebellion and Disobedience

Dr. Henry Brandt, the well-known Christian psychologist, made a penetrating statement regarding parenthood. He said a parent is "a partner with God in making disciples of their children."[7] Our methods of dealing with our children are to correspond with God's methods.

If you'll dwell on that long enough, it will begin to crystalize your attitude and your actions in the training of your children. All of us, in one way or another, are the disciples of our parents. Some have been more deeply impressed than others, but no one is completely removed from his home training.

Some of your habits (certainly some of the ways you as parents train your children), some of your weaknesses and some of your strengths go back to the way you were "discipled" as a child, as a youngster living under the roof of your guardian or parents. Parents' fingerprints are smeared all over the lives of their offspring.

Thus far we've been dealing with three very important phases related to raising children. We talked about *knowing your child*—making a study of him and going to great efforts to understand the way God has made him. Parents who want to be close partners with God in making disciples of their children must know each of them personally and intimately.

Next we talked about *loving your child*. This seems to be, of course, one of the great motivating factors for a happy life—that a child lives with love in the home.

Then, in the two previous chapters we discussed *training your child*. We found that telling isn't necessarily training. We also learned that unless great effort is made to inculcate the right standards into the inner lives of our disciples, they won't be able to stand alone. They will give in. Stability comes from good solid training.

Now, we need to think through some important issues

regarding *disciplining your child*. That makes sense. "Disciple" and "discipline" are derived from the same root word. A good disciple is well-disciplined. Many people feel that love for the child and discipline of the child are at odds with each other—that they are mutually exclusive, even enemies. Some teach if you really love your child, you won't *need* to discipline him. Or that if you discipline your child he will have every reason to doubt your love.

That's not true. As a matter of fact, in Prov. 13:24 we find just the opposite statement declared in Scripture: "He who spares his rod hates his son, But he who loves him disciplines him diligently."

I want to say something before I go any further. A clarification is needed. When we talk about disciplining and discipling our children, we're *not* talking about crushing their spirits. That's cruel and totally unbiblical. We are, however, talking about breaking and curbing their assertive self-wills. There's a great difference.

Massive, brutal force, sheer effort with an instrument of punishment will certainly force the child to sit down and be quiet. At least on the outside. But that also can crush his spirit. We're talking about using the rod *and* developing the child's character deep within.

The proverb we just read is saying, "If you really love the child, you will be diligent about disciplining him." I know as I write on the subject that I am treading on very delicate soil. I know it arouses hostile feelings in people who were mistreated and even in those who were not disciplined at all.

Look at the word *diligently*. Originally, this Hebrew word meant "dawn," "early morning." Later, it evolved into the idea of "something that was longed for early in the day." Then it came to mean the idea of going after something at an earlier age or pursuing something with a longing in the heart. Now we have the English term *diligent* as the translation of a word that originally meant "early" or "dawn." That is very significant because when we talk about correction for the children, we talk about something that should begin at a very early age.

In the Old Testament, there are two main words for correction—two major concepts.

This passage uses the first term. A transliteration of the actual Hebrew term would be *yahsaar*. "He who spares his rod hates his son; but he who loves him *yahsaars* him diligently." He pursues this with a longing in his heart. The word *yahsaar* means "to chastise." It implies the use of the rod. It means corporal punishment. It is a term that is rather harsh.

If it's all that we had in the Scripture, the process would be quite bleak. It suggests the idea of bringing oppression and physical pain to a person. It is what we commonly refer to as a spanking, "taking a licking" as they used to say.

Now, Prov. 13:24 teaches that the parent who loves his child disciplines him early. Proverbs 19:18 also makes that clear: "Discipline your son while there is hope, And do not desire his death."

There were occasions in the Old Testament when an older boy who was hopelessly beyond reform was publicly stoned to death. Capital punishment was provided for the older son who steadfastly refused the discipline of his parents. That explains why the proverb reads, "Don't desire his death."

Susanna Wesley, mother of Charles and John Wesley, is perhaps the classic illustration of one who pursued discipline early in the child's life. She believed the assertive self-will of a child must be broken by the parent early in life. She felt he should know by then that his will must yield to his parents' word and authority. One of her rules in her "plan of education" was:

> When turned a year old (and some before), they were taught to fear the rod and to cry softly, by which means they escaped abundance of correction which they might otherwise have had. . . . In order to form the minds of children, the first thing to be done is to conquer their will . . . .[8]

To the young man or lady reading this book, it makes your parents groan when they think about disciplining if they have failed to do as they should. It hurts a parent to realize that what the Scriptures really have been teaching has not been carried out. Do not go home and, over the lunch table, point out all your parents' failures to them. Many parents did not know what the Scriptures teach when they were raising their children. Your mom and dad may be learning while you are learning. We are *all* in the process of becoming disciples. Susannah Wesley's words are wise. The best time to start is when children are young.

Another thought that comes to mind when I think of pursuing discipline diligently is the matter of consistency. Something that was wrong yesterday is wrong today. Something that brought the rod last week should bring the rod this week. Consistency is perhaps the most important ingredient in proper discipline. We all wrestle with it. Face it; extremes come easy. Balance is hard to maintain. It's seen in our posture. We don't stand up straight—we lean or slump. We don't move calmly and smoothly through life—we ricochet!

So when it comes to consistent discipline, we blow it. It's our natural habit to volley back and forth between rigid regulation and broad permissiveness—with daily nagging and chiding and threatening in between. Our youngsters witness the swing of our pendulum from passive neglect to intense rigidity, then find themselves suddenly inundated with stacks of gifts, often given to silence our own guilt. What a trap! How confusing to children! God has a better idea . . . *yahsaar*.

Proverbs 22:15 is another passage using the Hebrew term. "Foolishness is bound up in the heart of a child; The rod of discipline will remove it far from him."

It deals with a problem and its solution. Notice that the first part of the proverb is the problem, and the second part is the solution. Most people will agree with the first part, but only a precious few will stick with the solution because it requires consistency. Even in Christian circles, there seems to be a lack of interest and emphasis on that second part.

First the problem: "Foolishness is bound up in the heart of a child." Take away the words "the heart of a child," place your child's name here; it applies! Now, when the Scripture mentions foolishness, it doesn't mean fun, lightheartedness, and a good sense of humor. In the Old Testament, a fool was one who despised discipline, one who hated wise instruction. A fool mocked God, was quarrelsome, licentious, morally bad, and wicked. (See Chapter 8 of this book, "You and Your Daughter," for a more complete treatment of foolishness in children.)

Now look at the latter part of Prov. 22:15. ". . . the rod of discipline will remove it far from him." Remove what? Foolishness—that tendency toward rebellion and disobedience and mockery. God could have told parents to use any other method. But He mentions "the rod." It may not be popular nor considered an appropriate method, but spankings—properly and consistently administered—will drive foolishness out of your child's life. There's the solution!

Look at Prov. 19:3. You'll see what happens to a son who is graduated from his home without the rod having done its work. "The foolishness of man subverts his way, And his heart rages against the Lord."

Do you have an older boy who is not interested in spiritual things today? It may be the result of your failure to apply consistent, and I might add, *painful* yet fair discipline when it was needed. As a result, when he came of age he rejected the things of God—the things that meant so much to you. He had no effective standard for determining what was right.

Look at Prov. 23:13 again: "Do not hold back discipline from the child [here is our word *yahsaar* again], Although you beat him with the rod, he will not die." He may cry as though he would die, but he will not die. When you use the rod and deal with him correctly and consistently, Scripture says you "deliver his soul."

Now, when we read the words "beat him with a rod" we usually conjure up the picture of a brutal beast of a father who pounds away on his son's flesh. Bill Cosby gets lots of laughs as he refers to his dad who threatened to "rip the meat off his body." That is certainly not the biblical idea of *yahsaar*.

A vital tool in the well-disciplined household is the rod. I heard of an evangelist who was raised by faithful parents who used the rod on him. It was a long board that hung beneath a small hand-painted sign. His mother had painted that sign which read, "I need thee every hour." He said that as he grew up, he didn't know whether she meant the Lord or the board. By the time he was grown and this rod had been applied to him throughout his years, he realized it meant both! Every time the paddle was used, it reminded him of how very much he needed the Lord.

When you read the words "beat him with the rod," you must realize it's talking about the use of an implement, a rod, for the sake of driving foolishness from the heart of the child. It's not talking about child-battering, I repeat. It disturbs me greatly when I read of people who refer to this Old Testament passage and say, "Here's another example of a person who uses something that's brutal and completely out of date." No!

As a matter of fact, this word *rod* is used eight times in the book of Proverbs, and every time it means, or has reference to, the application of discipline.

I was raised in a family where we were spanked. And I mean hard. The rod my dad used grew on the end of his arm—it was his hand. He was a machinist by trade and had quite a hand. I remember associating a good deal of fear with my father, but I didn't really know why. I was never really close to my dad. I feared him. Not because he was unfair but because he hurt, for one thing.

And I was a disobedient young fellow. I remember frequently the use of his hand on my person. And I recall when we had children, I began to do the same thing, and there began to be a gap brought on by the same fear. Then it dawned on me that Scripture never refers to striking the child with the *hand* when discipline is administered. Invariably, it uses the word *rod*.

I thought, "Boy, that sounds harsh." So I did a study in the original language and found that the rod literally means "club." I was very grateful that my father hadn't known this passage of Scripture. It means "stick." It means "staff." It means "weapon."

I decided it would be better for my wife and me to use an object that was not associated with us, that is, not a part of our bodies. We began to use a paddle about the size of a ping-pong paddle. The one we use most often has been glued a couple of times on the handle. It may not look like it does the job, but it really does.

We never strike our children on the face. A physician told me a number of years ago that it is a threat on a child's life to be hit on the face. God has provided a vast amount of flesh in an excellent area for the use of the rod. Neither the rod nor the hand belongs on the face. If God had wanted it to be a hand, He would have said "h-a-n-d." But all the way through Proverbs, the book on how to handle life at home, it's always the rod.

I have seen mothers and dads literally slap their children so hard they'd stagger backwards. That's not discipline; that's brutality. The Scriptures never refer to that as the ministry of the rod.

We have one of these paddles for each of the children. Onto our main paddle, my wife has glued the familiar prayer:

God grant me the courage to change the things I can change, the serenity to accept those I cannot change, and the wisdom to know the difference. But God, grant me the courage not to give up on what I think is right even though I think it is hopeless.

Our children, when they were younger, often hid the paddles. We found them in the most interesting places. It's our plan that when they reach adult life, we will give them their own paddle to be a reminder of those days at home in which we made every attempt to implement the right guidelines.

Several years ago, I spanked our youngest daughter with one of the paddles. As is our custom, I stayed with her and comforted her afterwards and assured her of my affection and my desire that she never disobey me like that again. Then I walked out. About ten minutes later, she cried out, "Daddy!"

It was bedtime and the room was dark. I walked back in and said, "What do you want, Honey?" She pointed to the paddle on her desk and said, "Get that thing out of here!" She had associated the act of discipline with the rod, not with me.

Take a look at a verse of Scripture—Lam. 3:19, 20 and 28. I ran across this passage some time ago and it made me laugh out loud.

> Remember my affliction and my wandering, the wormwood and bitterness. Surely my soul remembers [this one has been under affliction and he is thinking about the discipline—the child must be given time to think] And is bowed down within me. This I recall to my mind, Therefore I have hope.

Now look at verse 28: "Let him sit alone and be silent since He has laid it on him."

I can hear some of you laughing . . . unless you're the child. All right! So much for *yahsaar*.

Turn next to Proverbs 3 and let's look at the second Hebrew term, which is *yahkaag*. It sounds a little like the other word, but it's not the same.

Yahkaag is the word often used to describe God's action of discipline. It is a term that literally means "to prove," "to convince," "to convict," "to correct." It frequently involves instruction.

Discipline is not discipline (in the biblical sense of the word) if it's *just* the rod or a tongue-lashing. That's harassment. That doesn't put submission into a child nor does it drive out foolishness. It irritates, exasperates, and humiliates. That's why Col.

3:21 says:"Fathers, do not exasperate your children, that they
may not lose heart." There must be careful instruction *along
with* the administration of the rod or it becomes completely
misunderstood by the child.

God's method is described in Prov. 3:11: "My son, do not reject
the discipline of the Lord, Or loathe His reproof [*yahkaag*]." It is
translated here *reproof*. "For whom the Lord loves He reproves
[He convinces, He convicts, He proves to be wrong], Even as a
father, the son in whom he delights" (Prov. 3:12).

Yahsaar has to do with the outside, the outer activity, the
outer wrong, the outer overt disobedience. *Yahkaag* deals with
the inside. It supplies information and direction. In other words,
there must first be the establishment of a standard. That standard can't vacillate from year to year, from one part of the country
to the other, according to age, or whatever. The standard is the
standard.

It is essentially the father's job to establish standards. He
establishes the rules and regulations of home and delegates the
responsibility and authority to the mother, who carries out his
desires through the long hours when he may not be at home. This
doesn't necessarily mean that when dad comes home he must
administer all the discipline. It simply means he establishes the
limits; both are engaged in instruction. Instruction (or "reproof") establishes right and wrong in the mind of the child.
Don't forget that the father is pictured here as one who delights
in his son.

The word *delight* means "to be pleased with, to accept favora-
bly, to admire." Dads, delight in your children! When is the last
time you told your boy how much you delight in him? Come on,
honestly now, when is the last time you took your boy by the
arm—I don't care if he is thirty—and pulled him up close and told
him what a delight he is to you? When is the last time, after you
administered the rod, you pulled him close and told him how
much you delight in him? That child's spirit will not be crushed
nor his self-esteem damaged if your discipline is mixed with
genuine delight.

You see, a father or mother who really delights in each child
conveys that delight in the reproof. I say again that it breaks my
heart to think of how many children are whipped black and blue
with a sharp, stinging *tongue*. That's unfair. God has provided a

rod. The rod is to be administered not half-heartedly but severely in the proper place on the body. And at the proper time—between instruction and affection. It must be that way. That's reproof.

I have seen occasions where the child simply didn't know what he had done wrong. The rod was used, but the child was in a quandary. *Take the time to explain.* (It also gives you the occasion to calm down.) Then after the explanation, administer the rod like you mean it.

Parents, look at Prov. 15:4: "A soothing tongue [the word means "healing"] is a tree of life, But perversion in it crushes the spirit."

What is perversion? It includes sharp, bitter, ugly words as well as profanity. It grieves me to hear children cursed by their parents. I was in a grocery store recently where a mother was irritated by her son's disobedience. She glared at him and screamed an oath like I had not heard since the Marine Corps barracks. She let him have it with both barrels. She verbally tore him apart, limb by limb. Her tongue was a perversion.

The boy glared in her direction, unmoved, and cursed back. Was he disciplined? No way. The tongue, no matter how loud or how sharp, cannot do the work of a rod. A tongue of perversion crushes the spirit.

There is to be delight. There is to be instruction. There is to be a spirit of reasonableness in the administration of discipline. It's what we might call *disciplining with dignity*.

Look at Job 23 for a moment. Job was in the midst of affliction, and he longed for an audience with God. Why he wanted that is explained right here in this passage. Remember now, he is covered with boils. He's under the smarting rod of God, as it were. So he longs for an audience with the King of heaven. He says, in verses 3 and 4:

> Oh that I knew where I might find Him, That I might come to His seat! I would present my case before Him And fill my mouth with arguments [the word is *yahkaag*, yet it is rendered *arguments*; I think *reasonings* might be better].

"Lord, let's talk this over. Let's discuss this. I need some reasons to help me understand why I'm going through this." Verses 5-7 then state:

I would learn the words which He would answer, And perceive what He would say to me. Would He contend with me by the greatness of His power? No [look, fathers!], surely He would pay attention to me. There the upright would reason [*yahkaag*] with Him [we would talk it over]; And I would be delivered forever from my Judge.

What a beautiful expression of one enduring pain and affliction! Job saw God as One with Whom he could reason.

Father . . . Mother, is there a reasonableness in your heart when it comes to discipline? I'm not talking about hedging on the rod. If there is wrong, it must be dealt with. But would a discussion of the issues help clarify the problem? Is your child free to talk things over with you? The child who learns to respect the authority of the parents has little trouble respecting the authority of God.

It just makes sense. Your relationship with your disciple will, when he reaches adulthood, be turned into his relationship with his Lord. Thus the mother's and father's roles are very important in the development of the child's relationship with God. Reasonableness plays a vital part in that development.

A parent, for example, must not permit back talk. Whenever a child gives his parents "lip" he should be disciplined. No child should be allowed to sass his parents. Back talk must be discouraged—*but not all talk*. An unreasonable parent may easily discourage all talk, capping off vital communication. The wise, reasonable parent will do whatever is possible and right to encourage genuine discussion, which includes giving reasons, explanations, clarifications, and information as a child feels compelled to talk. The youngster may have a worthwhile point he ought to have the opportunity to express.

Proverbs 29:15 gives us beautiful balance. "The rod and reproof give wisdom. . . . (Here's the word again—*yahkaag*.) The rod, mixed with instruction, delight, and an understanding, reasoning spirit yield wisdom. You can't have wisdom without a proper mixture of both. There must be the rod, but there must also be reproof.

I went to elementary school with a boy I'll call Chet. I'll never forget him. Chet was the most disobedient, rebellious little guy in our whole class.

I sat right behind Chet in sixth grade. One morning I saw something on the back of his shirt that looked like blood. At recess I said to him, "You've got something on your shirt, Chet."

He said, "Yeah, I'll show you what I have on my shirt."

As he lifted his shirt I became nauseated. There were bright red welts all over his back. The blood had come to the surface of his skin as a result of his father's lashing him across his back with a thick leather belt. He told me all about it. I could hardly believe my ears. I remember trembling, shaking all over.

Chester became a hardened rebel, the toughest kid in our high school. He dropped out during the eleventh grade. The last I heard from him he was serving time in the state penitentiary. Wasn't Chester spanked? Wasn't he whipped? Yes. But there was no reproof . . . no reasonable instruction, no opportunity to talk things over with his parents. Chester grew up hating his dad and lacking wisdom. He was struck often by an angry father who was determined to beat that boy into shape. That's not discipline. That's disaster.

I want to explain the process my wife and I have developed in disciplining our children. Granted, they're young. But we have discovered a method that is working, and I'd like to pass it on to you.

First of all, whenever we administer discipline, it is always on the basis of prior instructions. As a father, I have made every effort to establish (after counsel and discussion with Cynthia) the standards for our home. Certain things are permissible; certain things are not. When we are in other people's homes or out in public, that standard is exactly the same. Our children understand that.

When there is willful disobedience, a breaking of the standard, when our prior instruction is refused, then we have a disciplinary encounter. And the encounter is *always held in private*. We may be at a grocery store. We may be on a trip. But you will never *see* us discipline our children. We make every effort of not doing it even in front of the other children. It's a threatening experience to watch discipline happen to someone else. So we take them aside. Alone.

We do not usually talk about *why* they disobeyed. That's an endless verbal excursion that easily leads to lying and rationalization. We talk about *what* was done. We quickly (and calmly, if possible) explain the precise act of disobedience. We spell out what they did wrong. Then we admonish them with the rod. We do not spank lightly. We do it strongly. We make sure we strike them on the right place without the cushion of a lot of clothing.

In the application of the rod, we do not allow the child to refuse to cry nor to scream in a wild rage. He knows that. When the child cries, he flushes out his guilt; he clears his conscience. But when a child screams with rage, he is expressing anger. We don't permit that.

On one occasion we had to spank one of our children *four* times. The first time for the disobedient act, the next three times for the rage until he cried softly.

You say, "Wow! That's unfair." No. That's biblical. It is also quite effective. It helps curb and break that stubborn assertive self-will. As soon as the discipline had ended, there was a submissive spirit. We do not quit until there is. Then love is instantly applied. Affection. Grief may show on our faces, but never is there the rejection of the child.

Never do we smack the child across the face and then walk out of the room. We stay with them. In the time we spend with them (occasionally as much as thirty minutes) we assure them of our love. We mention our desire that they never ever do that again. Once the encounter is ended, we do not mention it again. We never review it in public. It's over and done with.

You know what? I've noticed lately that our younger children, as soon as the discipline is administered and is over, turn and reach up. They don't turn around and run. They reach for our affection.

Little Chuckie, our smallest, has just begun to do that. When we spank his little behind, we get his attention very firmly. With a submissive spirit, he turns and comes to us. We hold him close. I've had our two younger ones smother me with kisses after the discipline and reproof. I've had them express apology to me. They know how much I love them. It occurs to me we've had to discipline them less now that we've gotten down to business and carried through in the manner I explained. For us, it's working.

You say, "Well, that sort of discipline takes time. I'm busy. Too busy to do all that. I'll be late getting to my appointment. I've got deadlines." Then be late. Sound idealistic? Impractical? It just depends where your priorities are. If you have in your heart the determination that the child you're going to present to society is going to have proper respect for authority, a submissive spirit, and assurance of his parents' love, then you'll pay whatever price is necessary. Frankly, few things are more important to my wife and me.

You see, if we as parents are in partnership with God making disciples of our children, there's no way we can ignore consistent, fair, reasonable discipline.

God doesn't.

7

You and Your Son

GOD, GIVE US MEN!

God, give us men! A time like this demands
Strong minds, great hearts, true faith and ready hands;
  Men whom the lust of office does not kill;
Men whom the spoils of office cannot buy;
  Men who possess opinions and a will;
Men who have honor; men who will not lie;
Men who can stand before a demagogue
  And damn his treacherous flatteries without winking!
Tall men, sun-crowned, who live above the fog
  In public duty and in private thinking;
For while the rabble, with their thumb-worn creeds,
Their large professions and their little deeds,
Mingle in selfish strife, lo! Freedom weeps,
Wrong rules the land and waiting Justice sleeps.[9]

Josiah Holland wrote those words near the end of the
nineteenth century . . . on the heels of a bloody civil war. It was
a dark, dreadful hour. During that time there was a desperate
need for such men in the city, in the state, in the nation, and in the
churches.

It's the same today. We too are living in days of political
intrigue, days in which we do not know whom to believe. Perhaps
you have prayed in your own way, "God, give us men . . . tall
men . . . godly men . . . gracious men of conviction . . . men of
integrity."

But the simple fact is, God gives us *boys*. He gives mothers and
dads sons to rear into such men. He gives us little fellows who
have all the makings down deep inside for the potential of which
Holland writes. It is in the hands of the parents that the deep
responsibility for character construction rests. Daughters are

equally important, of course, but I want to concentrate only upon sons in this chapter.

Once again, we'll be turning to the book of Proverbs, going from chapter to chapter, verse to verse. We want to use the zoom lens on this reliable book of wisdom to pinpoint some of the ways we can raise boys to become men of honor and honesty.

I suggest that from the book of Proverbs there are five specific areas in which parents can do a job of manly construction. Maybe your boy is ten, twelve, thirteen, perhaps sixteen years old. It isn't too late, believe me. The construction process can still be carried on. It won't be easy . . . but when you consider the alternative, you'll be motivated to hang in there.

Maybe you have just had the joy of having a little man born into your home and are feeling a surge of responsibility. Perhaps you have a house full of girls and just one boy. He's outnumbered living in that girl's dorm. It could be you've adopted a son or are serving as foster parents to a boy. He needs assistance. Whatever the situation, God has a word.

STANDING ALONE IN THE WORLD

First of all, in Prov. 1:10-16 we find the need to teach our sons the importance of standing alone in a world system that is contrary to a life of Christian character.

> My son, if sinners entice you, Do not consent. If they say, "Come with us, Let us lie in wait for blood, Let us ambush the innocent without cause; Let us swallow them alive like Sheol, Even whole, as those who go down to the pit; We shall find all kinds of precious wealth, We shall fill our houses with spoil; Throw in your lot with us, We shall all have one purse." My son, do not walk in the way with them. Keep your feet from their path, For their feet run to evil, And they hasten to shed blood.

In these verses the writer is addressing sons. They are saying, in effect, "Learn to stand alone." Notice three closely related commands:

Verse 10: Do not consent.

Verse 15: Do not walk in [their] way.

Verse 15: Keep your feet from their path.

He's not saying, "In case you come in touch with such temptations . . . ," because every young man does. He's saying, "When you *do* come in touch, do not yield. Stand alone."

The nineteenth-century Norwegian poet Isben said, "The strongest man on earth is the one who stands most alone." Proverbs 13:20 talks about the same thing.

He who walks with wise men will be wise,
But the companion of fools will suffer harm.

Sons become like the boys they spend their time with. Companions have an unbelievable impact. Peer pressure is relentless. Savage is a better word.

Parents, it is our job to teach our sons the importance of standing alone when surrounded by foolish error. In other words, it is our responsibility to set forth the truth of God and in the process convince our sons of the importance of His truth. When they're convinced, standing alone will be predictable.

I should clarify what I mean by standing alone. Here's what I *don't* mean. We are not to raise another generation of self-sufficient individuals who couldn't care less about others. That creates an unhealthy mentality of intolerance. What's worse, it breeds isolationism. I'm not encouraging the raising of sons who become isolated, but rather insulated.

As our sons grow up, they are to be acutely aware of others—concerned, compassionate, gracious gentlemen—and yet deep within embrace principles that are absolutely unbending. They are to see right and wrong—and call it correctly. They are to be uncompromisingly committed to the Lord Jesus Christ—and still very much in touch with the needs of the world about them. In Holland's words, "Sun-crowned men who live above the fog," yet all the while very much involved in shaping their surroundings. Not standing off but standing alone.

There are ways parents can help pull this off. For example, teach your children what *a good friend* really is. Draw from your own experience, as well as from various Scriptures, the qualities of wholesome companions. Write them down with your son. Work together on the list. Few children know *how* to choose friends. They usually choose those who are attracted to them, and often it's the wrong group. Teach your children the things they might look for in a person they want to call their friend.

Remind them also of *the consequences of wrong*. It is easy to believe in masquerades of that which is not from God. Satan habitually paints a beautiful picture as he shows you the beginning of sin. A New Testament writer calls it "the passing pleasures of sin" (Heb. 11:25). Sin certainly has its pleasures, but they pass quickly. It is our job to convince our children the consequences of sin are far worse than temporary pleasures which may come. If it's appropriate, feel free to share a few of the lessons you learned in your earlier years. He won't lose respect for you, mom and dad. It will help him realize you really do understand the struggle.

Psalm 73, written by a man named Asaph, does a good job of convincing us as parents that to envy the evildoer is a foolish fantasy. Psalm 73:2-3 begins the account with a scene all of us can identify with:

> But as for me, my feet came close to stumbling; My steps had almost slipped. For I was envious of the arrogant, As I saw the prosperity of the wicked.

Apparent success of the godless is a real magnet to the young eye which sees the popularity of the wrong crowd. He thinks, "Man, that would be great! That's the way to live!"

"Until," says Asaph (v. 17), "I came into the sanctuary of God; Then I perceived their end." Everything looked great on the outside until he was alone and got some perspective on ultimate reality. While he was in church one day he got his head together. It was then he realized things in the world system were not as good as they looked on the surface. Our sons need us to help paint the consequences on the canvas of truth.

Acquaint your son with *the biographies of men* of God in history. As we noted, Prov. 13:20 says those who walk with wise men will be wise. We become like those we think about, those we spend our time with. When was the last time you read to or gave your son a good book about a godly person? Boys have a built-in admiration for military leaders, popular athletes, and public figures. There's a stack of good books like this available today in Christian bookstores. Use them with your son. Give them as special gifts. By associating these principles with reading and daily experiences, the process of building toward Christian manhood will begin.

Here are the types of books and other literature we have found helpful and which our sons have enjoyed:

- Political statesmen of great integrity and ability
- Christian athletes and coaches
- Biographies of heroic Bible characters
  (a children's story Bible is a must)
- Men of profound bravery on the battlefield
- Inventors, musicians, educators, and scientists whose walks with God have been influential
- Stories of well-known Christians in professional careers
- Magazine articles about people of faith who withstood insuperable odds
- Missionaries whom God used in unique ways

SENSITIVITY TO INSTRUCTION

Along with the ability to stand alone, our sons need to learn what is involved in being open to God's counsel and reproof. Proverbs 3:11-12 talks about this sensitivity to instruction:

My son, do not reject the discipline of the Lord, Or loathe His reproof, For whom the Lord loves He reproves, Even as a father, the son in whom he delights.

It is the job of the parent, especially the father, to teach a son how to be sensitive to God. I'll tell you quite frankly, folks, your son will rise up and call you blessed if you develop in him a tender spirit toward the Lord.

Why? Because you will save him untold hours of grief and heartache. To do this he must learn early that it is not manly or masculine to be stubborn in God's eyes. Masculinity is not being impudent and surly and proud before God. One of the greatest, yet rarest, qualities of manhood is having a tender spirit before God.

There's not a woman I know who does not deeply respect in a man the quality of sensitivity to God. A woman listens to the man who listens to God. A woman wants a man who is indeed a man, but she looks also for that necessary gentleness within him. She wants him "tough and tender," as Joyce Landorf puts it.

This verse warns not to reject or loathe God's reproof. You can think of some in the Scriptures who have, can't you? Eli rejected

God's counsel when he ignored his sons' disobedience. He paid for it dearly. Gehazi was a servant of a godly prophet named Elisha. His stubborn, insensitive spirit brought significant consequences. Jonah went almost too far in his insensitivity to God. So did Peter—almost to the brink of despair. Achan also refused to listen to the counsel and reproofs of God. How can we teach our boys to listen to God's direction?

First of all, *teach them how to respond to your own counsel.* You teach them how to respond to your discipline, fathers. We talked about that at length in Chapter 6. We deal as severely with *attitudes* in our home as we do with actions. A sullen, stubborn spirit is dealt with as directly as an act of lying or stealing. The way you deal with your sons will, in great measure, determine how they will respond to the way God deals with them.

Secondly, *help them see the value of other people's correction.* Teach them the significance of the policeman on the corner, the teacher in the classroom. Help them learn the value of respecting an employer in the company they will work for one day. Teach them to consider the counsel of their boss, fellow students, and especially those who walk with the Lord.

Thirdly, *share a few shadows from your own lives*—the areas where God had to show you some things through your mistakes and hard knocks. As I mentioned, let your sons in on insights from your lives where you have failed and paid dearly for refusing to listen to God. Be sure you convey the benefits of maintaining a sensitive spirit, as opposed to being hot and cold.

A fourth lesson on this subject is found in Prov. 19:20: "Listen to counsel and accept discipline, That you may be wise the rest of your days."

Although this is addressed to sons, it implies parental involvement. The lesson we draw from that implication is clear. *Spend sufficient time in counsel with your sons.*

What an assignment! We parents are so busy we hate to miss one panel of a revolving door. But we must learn how to do it. Sufficient counsel takes sufficient time. Wisdom calls for it.

An interesting study was done in the city of Chicago among several thousand businessmen who willingly gave themselves a test. The study, sponsored by a secular corporation, was trying to discern some meaningful statistics in the amount of time spent between a father and his son beyond eating together and sleeping in the same home. An incredible result came to the surface. An average of *six minutes a week* was spent with each boy by each father! We can *never* teach our sons how to be responsive to their Lord in six minutes a week. It will take time. I plead with you: *change your schedule.*

DEALING WITH TEMPTATION

There is a third area: dealing with temptation. That's something the book of Proverbs hits very hard. Interestingly, there are only two realms of temptation mentioned specifically in Proverbs: (1) temptation aroused by the opposite sex, and (2) the temptation of strong drink. Look how Solomon counsels his son. Proverbs 5:1-5 teaches:

> My son, give attention to my wisdom, Incline your ear to my understanding; That you may observe discretion, And your lips may reserve knowledge. For the lips of an adulteress drip honey, And smoother than oil is her speech; [As embarrassing as it sometimes is, we need to teach our sons that those chicks on the street will be extremely attractive, will be extremely admirable on the surface, and that their lips will drop words that are just like honey. Their approach will be smoother than oil.] But in the end she is bitter as wormwood, Sharp as a two-edged sword. Her feet go down to death, Her steps lay hold of Sheol.

Once more, Solomon warns in Prov. 6:20: "My son, observe the commandment of your father, And do not forsake the teaching of your mother." What is the commandment's purpose? Verse 24— "To keep you from the evil woman, From the smooth tongue of the adulteress." Again, she is called one with a smooth tongue. She is appealing. The counsel is, "Don't desire her beauty in your heart." In other words, don't meditate on such things. Put those thoughts out of your mind. That's a hard-line approach, but it's best.

But wait. It isn't enough to say, "Boy, don't do that. You can't do this." Your son needs to know how to carry out the command. Tell him how *you* keep from doing it. Tell him how to spend his mental energy in the right areas. It will take some thought, some planning.

Again, *time*. Time in honest discussion. Listening. Rapping, as

they say. Just because a boy has been born into your home
doesn't mean he automatically knows how to handle an open offer
of sex. A man doesn't meet his first available one-nighter after he
has become a businessman; he meets her on the street or at
school. He picks up on quickie sex from those around him. Your
boy *will* learn the facts of life. It will be either from you or off the
street. What a wholesome place for your son to form his first
impressions about the beautiful gift of sex—from his parents.
Stop and think of the enduring dividends he will cash in the rest
of his life as a result of learning it from you, the one he most
respects.

One of the questions I often ask in dealing with young couples
preparing for marriage relates to the intimacies of marriage:
"Have your parents explained married sex to you from God's
point of view?" I could number on both hands, and no more, the
couples who have answered yes. The great majority of the Christian couples with whom I have counseled received *zero* information from their parents on the matter of sexual truth. Of course,
by then they knew the facts—but not from their parents.

Romantic love is one of the most beautiful facets of the earthly
experience God has provided for man, yet parents strangely
withhold the real truth from their children. It is our job to
become their source of information, so they might be able to
enjoy two benefits the rest of their lives. First, how to say no to
the constant temptation to yield to sensual immorality . . . and
second, how to implement a full spectrum of intimate love in their
marriages. We must teach our boys how to say no when there is
every occasion to say yes. This is especially true since the majority of his peers are saying yes instead of no.

Let me amplify the subject of sensual temptation. You and I
know that our sexual drive isn't initiated in the abdomen but
rather in the brain. The whole issue of temptation goes back to
our thought life. And thoughts are prompted by our senses—
visual stimulation especially, as well as what we hear or touch.
That explains why Jesus could talk about "committing adultery
in the heart." Adultery occurs in the head long before it occurs in
the bed.

Your son needs to understand that. It's because he doesn't that
he becomes a victim rather than a victor of lust. My point? Your
boy needs help and ideas on how to control his thoughts. He will

never ask you, but he is ready to listen. He would love to know how to live and relate to the opposite sex without guilt.

Help him know, for example, the damaging effects of pornography. Instruct him on what to read and *not* to read . . . not even a glance. Discuss as well the films that are hindrances to his thought life—*and why.* Do this calmly and intelligently. Don't "talk down." Don't preach. Try not to come across like gangbusters. We have a saying in our home where we talk about "killing a roach with a shotgun." Overcoming temptation is a continual battle of the flesh. Make that clear to your son. Encourage him to share with you times when the battle is raging. Assure him of your absolute support and understanding. That helps keep the door open. It's a verbal green light saying, "Come back anytime you want to talk." Remember, you must keep his words confidential.

Of course, a challenging program of mutual Scripture memorization is a great offensive weapon. Notice I say "mutual." You do it with him. Choose verses that encourage pure thoughts. You might even listen to a set of cassette tape recordings together on the subject of handling temptation. Several are available. Ask your local bookstore for a list. Through all of this, of course, you want your son to realize that sex of itself is not dirty nor sinful. In the right setting (marriage) and with the right person (his wife), it's sheer delight. Absolute bliss. Emphasize that!

Then there is the other area mentioned in Proverbs: strong drink. With the allurement of attractive magazine ads and enormous billboard advertisements around us, I think if a boy went by what he heard and saw, he would be led completely down the primrose path as far as alcohol is concerned. Again, it's our job as parents to teach him *how* to handle it.

Solomon says in Prov. 23:19-21:

> Listen, my son, and be wise, And direct your heart in the way. Do not be with heavy drinkers of wine, Or with gluttonous eaters of meat; For the heavy drinker and the glutton will come to poverty, And drowsiness will clothe a man with rags.

"It may look attractive, son, but you will be a ragged old man if you continue in this vein." He continues in verses 29-35:

> Who has woe? Who has sorrow? Who has contentions? Who

has complaining? Who has wounds without cause? Who has redness of eyes? Those who linger long over wine, Those who go to taste mixed wine. Do not look on the wine when it is red [how about that counsel?], When it sparkles in the cup, When it goes down smoothly;[He read the "billboards" in his day, didn't he? He heard what the people were saying.] At the last it bites like a serpent, And stings like a viper. Your eyes will see strange things, And your mind will utter perverse things. And you will be like one who lies down in the middle of the sea, or like one who lies down on the top of a mast. [This is a picture of foolishness once a person is drunk. Then he describes the testimony of one.] "They struck me, but I did not become ill; they beat me, but I did not know it. When shall I awake? I will seek another drink."

Here is the miserable, painfully familiar syndrome. It's the whirlpool in which a person is caught who does not know how to handle the problems and temptations of strong drink. Do you realize you cannot take an airplane trip, attend a banquet, a play, a business or promotional meeting, a dinner in the evening, a celebration in the secular world, a cruise at sea, a sales gathering, or a military party, without having the issue of virtually unlimited alcohol splashed before you on every hand? Think now: How will your boy know how to respond if *you* do not instruct him? This help on overcoming temptation is the responsibility that rests especially with the fathers. Start early!

Not long ago there was a program on television entitled "The Young Alcoholic." I discovered from that particular program that in the Greater Los Angeles area there are a million people between the ages of twelve and twenty. Three-fourths of them have used alcohol, according to that report. In fact, seventy-five hundred of them in Los Angeles County are alcoholics! Twenty-five percent of Alcoholics Anonymous' time is spent with those in that age bracket.

The incredible thing to me was how amazed most of the parents were, how they denied the reality of the problem until the child himself told them. In fact, some children are drinking by the fourth grade, according to the program. In case you haven't stopped to figure, that's a nine- or ten-year-old child.

I am not asking you to become a negativistic type of person.

I'm asking you to be realistic, to set the record straight. If you
don't, nobody will. You establish either a corrective therapy or a
preventive therapy in the home. Either you deal with your son
now or after he's trapped. That is said from a pastor's perspective; Christian kids are not immune. Try it, because the voice
that says, "It's exciting and wonderful and rewarding. You only
go around once. Enjoy!" is far stronger and more persuasive than
the voice saying, "It's not worth it. It will sting like a viper. The
consequences are tragic. Watch out!"

Dealing with temptation is not automatic. It is a series of
practical techniques that must be passed on from father to son.
The best place on earth for this relay of truth to occur is in the
home.

MONEY

Teaching your son how to handle finances is a crucial fourth
issue in Proverbs. Notice in Prov. 3:9-10 that Solomon talks
about finances: "Honor the Lord from your wealth, And from the
first of all your produce; So your barns will be filled with plenty,
And your vats will overflow with new wine."

Solomon is speaking to his son when he says, "Learn how to
invest your money in the things of the Lord."

The subject of finances covers four areas: teaching a boy how
to *give*, how to *earn*, how to *spend*, and how to *save*.

Solomon says the child is to learn first the joy of giving to the
Lord. He learns this from his parents by seeing it happen in their
lives. When it comes to money in general, remember the principle stated in Prov. 22:7, 9:

The rich rules over the poor, And the borrower becomes the
lender's slave. . . . He who is generous will be blessed, For he
gives some of his food to the poor.

It begins in most homes with an allowance. Maybe your boy is
just old enough to start receiving an allowance. Let's say he
receives one dollar a week. Take the time to tell him how to
receive those one hundred pennies and use them wisely. (The
value is getting less and less as time moves on!) Train him to start
small and build.

A Christian friend of mine in Denver, Colorado, has several

children. Some time ago they faced a real financial problem: there
was just not enough money to go around in the family. His kids
got an idea. There was an empty lot next door. They checked
with the owner, and he said it was fine for them to use it. So they
plowed it up and grew corn, enough to make a little money—in
fact, just enough money that first summer to encourage them to
do the same thing the next summer.

The following year the daughter in that family wanted to go
with her dad to the Orient, but it would take almost $800 to make
the trip there and back, all expenses included. Neither of them
had that kind of money.

She said, "I'll tell you what. I'll find another lot to take care of
all by myself."

He said, "Fine." But they all pitched in.

They found a much larger lot elsewhere, and these kids began
farming.

He told me, "I've never farmed in my life, but we got the
necessary equipment, rolled up our sleeves, and started in."
Later they set up a stand, got some bushel baskets and filled
them with corn. They couldn't keep them filled. They sold everything they raised that summer. And sure enough, his daughter
was able to pull herself out of school for three or four weeks to go
with her dad to the Orient, using the money the family had
raised. What a memory for that family to recall!

That's not all. They sat down together that next winter and
realized they had a going thing. They thought ten years ahead
when four or five children would be gone. They had only ten
years to teach them how to handle their money. The father of
that family is a wise man. Those kids are really learning how to
handle money.

Think creatively and uncover some projects to help your boy
know the value of giving and some of the secrets of saving.
Solomon says the one who borrows constantly becomes a slave to
the one who lends constantly. Rare indeed will be your boy if he is
raised to know how to handle his money.

HARD WORK

All this leads me to the fifth and final area. We've thought
about standing alone, being sensitive, dealing with temptation,

and handling money. Let's complete the chapter with an emphasis on working hard.

Proverbs 10:4, 5 says:

> Poor is he who works with a negligent hand, But the hand of the diligent makes rich. He who gathers in summer is a son who acts wisely, But he who sleeps in harvest is a son who acts shamefully.

Those two verses say *it pays off*. If he listens to all his buddies, your boy may be hearing, "The ignorant work, the smart get by without it." God says, "The one who is the happiest is the one who has learned the value of hard work." What on earth has become of two-fisted work in our cultural climate? Most of us are ready to go to bed over a hangnail. Some college students, before they graduate and get a job, think manual labor is the president of Mexico.

Proverbs 13:4 says:

> The soul of the sluggard craves and gets nothing,
> but the soul of the diligent is made fat.

Your soul—the real you down inside—prospers if you work hard. Working hard is a rewarding joy.

The best counsel my father ever gave me upon graduating from high school was to *learn a trade*. So for the next four and a half years I went into a machine shop and worked during the day, attending school at night in pursuit of the academic phase of my life. As a machinist's apprentice I learned endless, valuable lessons about hard work before I graduated from that program as a journeyman machinist. Hardly a week passes that I don't give thanks in some measure for learning a skill that requires working with my hands. It also gives me an empathy for the man of this world who grinds out a hard day's labor day after day after day.

Are you going to school? Try to work as well as go to school. What do you tell your boy? "That's okay, Son, I'll cover it. That's all right, I'll pay for it. I'll pick up the tab. Don't worry about that, Son, I'll take care of it. Here, here is the credit card; put it on my account." A strange creature emerges from a home like that. He's usually lazy and indifferent. Getting something for nothing prompts irresponsibility.

Or do you say, "It's time for you to earn your own way." That
boy will look back and thank God that you taught him the value of
hard work. So will his future wife.

Beyond these five items of advice, your boy must be very
aware that *you love him*. He will never be too old for that. When
is the last time you took him in your arms and held him close so no
one else could hear, and you whispered to him how happy you are
to have him as your son?

A show of emotion—is that effeminate? I'll be frank with
you—that's a sign of a great man. A man who can pull his boy
aside and say, "My life would not be the same if I lost you; my life
has been transformed now that you've come into our home; you
have no idea of what you have meant to me as a dad," is a man who
will reproduce himself in his son. More than likely he will become
one of those men of "strong minds, great hearts, true faith, and
ready hands," as Holland put it.

Great dads, you see, raise great sons. I memorized this
anonymous poem years ago. It says it all:

There are little eyes upon you,
And they are watching night and day;
There are little ears that quickly
Take in every word you say.

There are little hands all eager
To do everything you do;
And a little boy who's dreaming
Of the day he'll be like you.

You're the little fellow's idol;
You're the wisest of the wise;
In his little mind, about you
No suspicions ever rise.

He believes in you devotedly;
Holds that all you say and do,
He will say and do in your way
When he's grown up just like you.

There's a wide-eyed little fellow
Who believes you're always right;
And his ears are always open,
And he watches day and night.

You are setting an example
Every day in all you do;
For the little boy who's waiting
To grow up to be just like you.

The greatest contribution of all is to have the joy of looking back and saying, "I led my son to a knowledge of Jesus Christ and to the delight of walking in His steps." Do not delay in getting some time alone with your boy, even if it takes an entire day every week or two. Develop a relationship in his life that is meaningful, memorable, and will never end.

Never.

8
You and Your Daughter

"I would give everything we have today for two godly daughters . . . everything." The mother who spoke was a middle-aged wife of an eminently successful businessman. They were heavily endowed with this world's goods. It seemed that everything they touched turned to gold. Except their daughters.

The older one was, at that time, living a promiscuous life. An abortion, a marriage that had ended in divorce, and a non-Christian lifestyle had caused her parents indescribable grief. Her younger sister was following in her steps. There were evidences of drugs; she ran with a fast crowd. She was on the brink of dropping out of high school. The domestic scene was a study in contrasts. They had everything money could buy. What they longed for money *could not* buy. Peace. Sleep. Joy. Communication. Kindness. Godliness. The mother meant what she said. But she knew that no amount of money could purchase the priceless treasure of two daughters who walked with God.

I remember thinking, as that broken mother poured out her heart to my wife and me, "I wish I could wave a magic wand over this home and bring those girls back." But that's not God's approach. He tells us how to sow the right seeds so we can reap the right harvest. In His Word He spells out all the counsel we need to raise our daughters correctly.

We want to get some light on that very subject in this chapter. I can tell you before we go any further, the buck is going to stop with the daughter's mom and dad. I hope you're ready!

Certainly, even though I have two daughters, I don't have all the answers. I have, however, made a rather lengthy study of God's book on earthly wisdom—Proverbs. It's been enlightening to find how frequently the book mentions women and daughters. For the sake of clarity I would like to limit our thoughts to six types of daughters—three sets of contrasting characters.

First, there is the foolish woman as opposed to the wise.

Second, there is the contentious woman as opposed to the gracious. Third, there is the sensuous woman as opposed to the virtuous. Let's take them in that order as we attempt to glean insight on how to raise our daughters.

FOOLISH OR WISE

Consider the words of Prov. 14:1:

The wise woman builds her house,
But the foolish tears it down with her own hands.

Because the word *foolish* appears so often in Scripture, we need to understand its full meaning. Literally, the Hebrew term means "dull, thick, sluggish." Its use in this passage is no exception. The foolish woman of Prov. 14:1 is thick, dull, and sluggish to the things of God. Foolish women were once foolish daughters who were not changed in the process of growth. A foolish woman does not just all of a sudden *appear*. Foolishness has been there for years. It has been cultivated.

This verse describes a characteristic of a foolish gal. She is bent on destruction. She tears down her home with her own hands. (She evidently doesn't need a lot of help doing it!)

The term *tears down* come from a single Hebrew word meaning "to overthrow, to destroy." Her destructive bent was never curbed. She habitually overthrows that which is good.

An uncomfortable question hangs in your head: "How do I know if I have a foolish daughter?" Some tell-tale clues are mentioned elsewhere in Proverbs. Let's check them out so you can know the answer to your question.

Proverb 9:13 introduces the first clue: "The woman of folly is boisterous, She is naive, and knows nothing."

Actually, the verse is referring to a foolish girl. She is boisterous. That doesn't mean energetic or excitable—it means she is in constant commotion and turbulence. Literally, the Hebrew text conveys the idea of having a negative and tumultuous attitude.

Verse 17 adds more:

"Stolen water is sweet; And bread eaten in secret is pleasant."

That's what she says to her companions. She makes a mockery of sin, being thick and dull in her conscience. Her philosophy of life is a "white is black, hot is cold" mentality. She is a mistress of

deceit. She can look at you eyeball to eyeball and tell you a lie in
the most convincing manner. This is all part of her ability to
"mock at sin" (Prov. 14:9).

A final clue appears in 20:3:

Keeping away from strife is an honor for a man,
But any fool will quarrel.

The Hebrew term translated *quarrel* means "to burst forth in a
rage, a tantrum." A foolish daughter is argumentative and given
to rage. That's terribly vivid, but it's the truth.

Now think about your daughter. First, is she in constant
turbulence, showing a negative attitude, filled with uneasiness
and commotion? Second, is she deceptive, given to frequent
lying? Third, does she make a mockery of sin and guilt? Fourth, is
she, more often than not, quarrelsome and argumentative?

"Aw, Chuck, these are just normal for a girl growing up. Back
off, man. You're nitpicking." Maybe that's the way you feel.

My answer is—no, they aren't normal characteristics of a girl
whose life is being shaped by God. They are the natural characteristics of a girl whose bent is "foolishness." Let her continue in
that bent and you will give her hand to some future groom who
will face a lifetime of misery. The "bent" will be set.

Forgive me if all this sounds hard line. It is not meant as
harshness; it is sent forth as truth. In a book such as this, unless I
"call them as I see them," what I say will be of little help. Beyond
that, remember that as much as is humanly possible, I am not
offering Chuck Swindoll's child-cure potion. These truths are
God's analyses of some deep and serious matters. If there were
any way I could communicate the truth without coming across so
strong, believe me, I would.

Well, is there any hope for parents with foolish daughters?
Again, I must be frank. The outlook is rather bleak but not
hopeless. Look at Prov. 17:21: "He who begets a fool does so to
his sorrow, And the father of a fool has no joy."

Certainly, the longer we allow the bent to go untouched, the
worse the picture gets. And simply talking with her is not going
to do the job. Several proverbs (15:5; 18:2; 24:7) make it clear that
mere talk is virtually a waste. We do know from our study on
discipline that the rod of discipline will help remove foolishness
(22:15). A similar thought is in Prov. 26:3: "A whip is for the

horse, a bridle for the donkey, And a rod for the back of fools."

My counsel would be to pray specifically that God would sovereignly step in and change your daughter's bent. Also, parents, you *must* be consistent in the use of the rod, especially if your daughter is young and given to fits of temper or acts of deception. Deal strongly and severely with lies. The same goes for her argumentativeness. If you do not, you will live to curse the days you overlooked those bents.

Who knows? God in sovereign grace might send to your daughter or family another Christian who can minister in love, power, and reproof in your daughter's life.

Not too many months ago I was involved in a family whose daughter was in this category. After prayer mixed with heated and confronting discussions with her, she was struck with a sudden awareness of her foolish bent. She looked at her mother and they communicated volumes without a word. They all broke down in tears, and she said, deeply shaken, "I can remember when my stubborn streak started. I realize now how ugly and foolish I have been. Please, please forgive me."

God pulled it off. He can do the same with you and your foolish daughter. He is a Specialist when it comes to miracles.

Proverbs 14:1 also mentions her counterpart—the "wise woman." In contrast to the foolish, she "builds her house." She is constructive, one who builds rather than tears down.

This word *wise* or *wisdom* fills the book of Proverbs. Literally, it means "favorable." She looks at life from God's vantage point. She's a rare, rich jewel, according to Prov. 31:10-31. In my opinion this is the finest insight on the wise woman in all recorded history. Look at the first part of the passage:

> An excellent wife, who can find? For her worth is far above jewels. The heart of her husband trusts in her, And he will have no lack of gain. She does him good and not evil All the days of her life. She looks for wool and flax, And works with her hands in delight (Prov. 31:10-13).

She is rare.
She is trustworthy.
She is diligent.
She is committed to the family's well-being.
It's remarkable how much you can tell about a woman by

looking at her hands. She can doctor up her hair and face and do a beautiful job of adorning her body . . . but her hands tell a story all their own. This passage in Proverbs 31 tells us the wise woman works with her hands—and she does it *willingly.* She delights in it. A woman's hands will often reveal if she is a "wise woman."

The next several verses add to those lists of characteristics. She knows how to handle money. Teach your daughter that for sure. Her husband will *love* you for it in years to come! She thinks and plans ahead, she is secure and industrious, and she is kind in her speech. What a rare gem of lasting beauty!

My favorite expression of all in this superb section of Scripture is that statement in verse 25:

Strength and dignity are her clothing. . . .

Wow! What a spectacular picture of the wise woman! Her inner attire is woven from two balls of exquisite yarn—strength of character and dignity of manner.

Set some goals with your daughter this year. Work out some objectives with her, using this passage as a guide. That's how you can cultivate wisdom in your daughter. She will be forever grateful as she builds her future home.

CONTENTIOUS OR GRACIOUS

Proverbs 19:13 is funny and pathetic at the same time: "A foolish son is destruction to his father, And the contentions of a wife are a constant dripping." Drip . . . drip . . . drip . . . drip . . . .

"It is better to live in a corner of a roof, Than in a house shared with a contentious woman" (Prov. 21:9).

"It is better to live in a desert land, Than with a contentious and vexing woman" (Prov. 21:19).

Man! Now one more.

"A constant dripping on a day of steady rain and a contentious woman are alike; He who would restrain her restrains the wind, And grasps oil with his right hand" (Prov. 27:15-16).

Listen, friends and neighbors, Solomon knew what he was talking about. He had (are you ready for this?) seven hundred wives plus three hundred concubines. That's one thousand females to deal with. One thousand! If my figuring is right, it took him a little less than three years to make the rounds. I'd say he was something of an authority on contentiousness! When he writes about it, we'd better listen.

What does it mean to be contentious? The Hebrew term means "given to strife, easily angered." We would say "one who is a nag." It's the picture of one who picks a fight just for the love of fighting or nagging. Like a continual drip . . . drip . . . drip, it brings misery.

We've all met people like this. (It's not found exclusively among women, by the way.) A contentious wife came to me for counsel some time back. In several ways she conveyed the feeling that she really didn't want counsel as much as she wanted *agreement*.

It so happened I didn't agree with her. She became insistent. I calmly stood my ground and explained why. She stayed on her point, and stayed on it, and stayed on it . . . until the point was getting dull. I told her I really did not agree and in my opinion she was making a wrong decision.

She stood to her feet, grabbed her purse, stated her point once more, and stomped out. "I'm so glad I'm not married to you," I thought as she left in a cloud of dust.

Suddenly I was seized with the reality that some poor fella is. He lives with her nagging every day.

Proverbs pictures the contentious woman (wife or daughter) in that condition as a result of two particular problems. First, a daughter is contentious because her assertive self-will has never been broken. The root word translated *contentious* suggests the opposite of submissive, ruled, obedient, and governed. She *lacks* these qualities. If your daughter is showing signs of becoming a contentious young woman, work on her will! Point out your concern for her future. Counsel and discipline her faithfully.

Second, often a daughter is contentious because her mother is contentious. Like begets like, all things being equal. A mother with an unbroken self-assertive will has difficulty curbing a daughter like herself. That situation calls for a very loving and patient—yet firm husband/father to face the facts and work out a plan for change in habits of the home. To be painfully direct, it occasionally takes a calamity to break that syndrome. God must, in some cases, perform a supernatural work of grace in their hearts. The truth is, contentious women and daughters (and men too, for that matter) are often the heartbreak and heartache of many Christian pastors and churches. May God give great wisdom and grace as he brings about change and healing!

Well, there's a brighter side—the gracious woman. Proverbs 11:16 is an encouraging verse: "A gracious woman attains honor . . . ."

To be gracious means "to show consideration and acceptance." If I could sum up the truth of several proverbs on the gracious daughter, she reveals her condition in three ways—through her *lips*, her *appearance*, and her *attitude*.

Two specific actions characterize the gracious girl. First, she is *a person of appreciation*. Second, *she communicates this in thoughtful, tangible ways*. She is one who encourages others with words and gifts of gratitude.

The church I serve here in Fullerton has an abundance of gracious daughters and women. Our pastoral staff is often encouraged by these people who never run out of ways to show their appreciation. Hardly a week passes without one or more of us receiving a note of thanks—most often from these gracious ones who attain honor before God. They lighten our load immeasurably.

May their tribe increase!

SENSUOUS OR VIRTUOUS

Proverbs 2:16 is the first reference in the book to the "strange woman." Before we look at this and other related passages, let's understand what is meant by the biblical term *strange*. It means one who has become immoral, sexually promiscuous. The Hebrew term means "estranged, alienated." It suggests the idea of "separated" or "foreign." Perhaps she was seen as one who chose to separate from the accepted lifestyle of an Israelite woman. Whatever, the term found in Proverbs means a sensuous, morally loose girl or woman.

Look first at three different passages:

To deliver you from the strange woman, From the adulteress who flatters with her words; That leaves the companion of her youth, And forgets the covenant of her god; For her house sinks down to death, And her tracks lead to the dead; None who go to her return again, Nor do they reach the paths of life (Prov. 2:16-19).

For the lips of an adulteress drip honey, And smoother than oil is her speech; But in the end she is bitter as wormwood, Sharp as a two-edged sword. Her feet go down to death, Her steps lay hold of Sheol. She does not ponder the path of life; Her ways are unstable, she does not know it (Prov. 5:3-6).

For the commandment is a lamp, and the teaching is light; And reproofs for discipline are the way of life, To keep you from the evil woman, From the smooth tongue of the adulteress. Do not desire her beauty in your heart, Nor let her catch you with her eyelids. For on account of a harlot one is reduced to a loaf of bread, And an adulteress hunts for the precious life (Prov. 6:23-26).

If you were to go back over those vivid sections of Scripture to find the characteristics of a sensuous daughter, your first observation would be: *She is given to verbal flattery.* She speaks smoothly. Her words entice and persuade.

Parents, it is necessary that you listen to your daughter. Not just when she talks to you but others as well. Dads, it would be helpful for you to explain to your daughter how to communicate with fellas. You can help her recognize those words or actions which could appear inappropriate or suggestive.

A daughter with a sensuous bent will also be *overly interested in external beauty.* Now, of course, every teenaged girl is sensitive to her appearance; that is not unnatural nor wrong. But these proverbs describe a strong habitual preoccupation with the externals.

Another factor to look for will be her *desire to run with girls much older than she.* That seems to be an acceptable meaning of leaving the "companion of her youth" (2:17). A daughter who suddenly breaks off her relationship with lifetime chums to establish a relationship with fellas and gals considerably older than she should be questioned. It is a sign that merits her parents' attention.

Of course, by forgetting "the covenant of her God" (2:17), the daughter is *cooling off to spiritual things.* And that is never a healthy sign. It could be the beginning of sensuality . . . or something else entirely. No matter. Probe into the reason.

One final observation of the sensuous daughter we could draw from Scripture is tucked away in Prov. 7:6-12:

For at the window of my house I looked out through my lattice, And I saw among the naive, I discerned among the youths, A young man lacking sense, Passing through the street near her corner; And he takes the way to her house, In the twilight, in the evening, In the middle of the night and in the darkness. And behold, a woman comes to meet him, Dressed as a harlot and cunning of heart. She is boisterous and rebellious; Her feet do not remain at home; She is now in the streets, now in the squares, and lurks by every corner.

Note that she is *dressed as a harlot.* Solomon does not bother to amplify that, which is noteworthy. Men, being men, know what attire that is. What it was in Solomon's day was different than it is today. I don't want to dwell simply on the negatives, but this point needs more than a passing glance.

Your daughter communicates an enormous amount of information regarding her character by the way she dresses. Once again, dads are so important. Your daughter, especially as she begins to develop into a young woman, needs your wise counsel on her attire. Please be candid with her. Help her see that the way she looks in her clothing says far more than what she says with her mouth.

I honestly believe a growing daughter needs warmth, affection, communication, and even healthy embraces from her father on a regular basis. The same is true, of course, between a mother and her son. Families, unfortunately, have stopped hugging and exhibiting a show of affection. We're into a generation of touch-me-not families . . . and I have many reasons to believe it's unfortunate. Will you join me in helping break down that wall in families? I know of nothing else more effective in building a solid, stable standard of healthy affection among our children.

The virtuous woman is a wonderful change of subject. She appears in Prov. 12:4: "An excellent wife is the crown of her husband, But she who shames him is as rottenness in his bones."

The term *excellent* literally means "to be firm, strong, capable, efficient." It's the picture of a woman with strength of character . . . a virtuous person. It's a beautiful picture of feminine stability. It's one who walks a godly path, thinks godly thoughts, and carries out godly pursuits.

The world system could lead a daughter to believe this poor creature is chained to a stove or ironing board, frustrated and unfulfilled as a half-dozen kids are yanking on her soiled apron. Not so, according to Solomon! That's a straw man (or woman) erected by the propaganda from the world system.

Remember the words "strong, capable, efficient"? Literally, that's what the virtuous or excellent daughter really is. That's why she's a crown to her husband. No husband in his right mind wants a spineless echo, an unthinking vanilla shadow shuffling through the house. He wants one who "crowns" his life, someone who surrounds him with her inner beauty, who adorns his life with gems of efficiency and strength, who adds sparkle and depth and delight to the home. That's the kind of daughter our friend would have given anything to have. Who wouldn't? She is priceless.

Well . . . there you have it. That's enough food for thought to chew on for the next several months. May I make a final suggestion? Instead of just laying the book aside right now, thumb back over the chapter and call to mind the six different types of daughters we've been thinking about.

As you roll them over in your mind, before you go to sleep tonight, think about you and your daughter. Then ask God for His wisdom and courage as you begin to work with her.

You know what? He will give it to you.

9

Those Extra-Special Children

All children are special. As we have learned from Psalm 139, our children are prescribed from birth—they are all "prescription babies." That makes them special. Our children come to us as tiny "transplanted olive shoots," according to Psalm 128. They are individual persons with unique bents and characteristics, as we saw in Chapters 1 and 2. That also makes all children special.

As I'm writing these words, our youngest, Chuckie, is curled up on the sofa in our den with his rabbit. He has put on the well-worn record by Bill and Gloria Gaither and is singing softly:

When Jesus sent you to us, we loved you from the start
You were just a bit of sunshine from heaven to our hearts.
Not just another baby, 'cause since the world began,
There's been something very special for you in His plan.
    That's why He made you something special,
    You're the only one of your kind,
    God gave you a body and a bright healthy mind;
    He had a special purpose
    That He wanted you to find,
    So He made you something special
    You're the only one of your kind.[10]

Yes, all children are special. There's no one else quite like that little blond-haired guy in there with his rabbit. The same, of course, could be said of your child. Even the internal pattern, the genetic structure, varies from child to child, adding further evidence that each is special.

But some are *extra* special. Some children, because of unusual circumstances during the prenatal period or at birth—or afterward—are marked off by the Lord as extremely special gifts. Those very special gifts from God's heart to our home require from their parents an extraordinary amount of time, love, understanding, and attention. But the rewards are immeasurable.

In this chapter I want us to consider what God says about six extra-special types of children: the unplanned child, the adopted child, the handicapped child, the gifted child, the hyperactive child, and the one-parent child. We'll be thinking about each of these extra-special children from the viewpoint of Scripture, but our repeated emphasis will be on the *parents' attitude*. Therein lies the key to acceptance of your child and happiness in your home.

I have observed a curious phenomenon concerning attitudes within many families. It is a remarkable study in contrasts. When it comes to business matters, vacations, hobbies, or other pursuits of interest to mom and dad, there is immediate, active, and financial involvement.

But when it comes to the acute needs of children in those same families, I am appalled at the passivity of parents (particularly fathers) because "it's too much trouble," or "it's too expensive," or "it's nothing to be concerned about." This plague of passivity includes dental checkups, allergies, acne, persistent learning difficulties, hearing and visual problems, annual physical exams, and obvious hyperactive characteristics. I realize it may be costly, troublesome, and demanding to pursue the solutions, but who can measure the ultimate benefits?

THE UNPLANNED CHILD

The unplanned child is not necessarily unwanted or unloved, though occasionally those feelings accompany such births. If parents are wise, they will accept the little "surprises" as extra-special arrows for their quiver. Initially, this may be difficult—especially if the child's arrival is, from the parents' perspective, untimely.

Hidden away in the Old Testament book of First Chronicles is an obscure account of an untimely birth. It brought grief to the mother.

And Jabez was more honorable than his brothers, and his mother named him Jabez saying, "Because I bore him with pain" (1 Chron. 4:9).

We wish we knew more about Jabez. We do know some things, however, and none of those details are very pleasant. His mother named him Jabez, which meant "pain, sorrowful." Why? Because of some unrevealed tragic circumstance before his birth that cast a shadow upon his arrival.

It is a known fact that parental influence can greatly affect the nature of a child, and little Jabez did not escape that pessimistic influence. Frankly, his coming added increased pressure to an overburdened mother.

We don't know what caused the painful situation in his home. Perhaps there were already too many children for the mother to handle. It might have been brought on by extreme financial burdens. Maybe the father died after Jabez was conceived. Or the mother could have been ill and his arrival was simply the last straw. Whatever, the boy came into a home quite possibly unplanned and unwanted. His mother's feelings were clearly discernible by the fact she named him Jabez—*pain*! A trace of bitterness and resentment, no doubt.

I understand a little of what Jabez must have struggled with. My mother told me from my earliest years that I was unplanned. I distinctly remember her using the words "unwanted" and "mistake." As a little fella, I felt uneasy because of that sense of burden I brought into the home. I recall one of her most often-repeated statements: "I'll be so glad when you kids are twenty-one."

I honestly believe she loved us. She certainly cared for my physical needs. But small children bothered her. It was an unfortunate situation, though certainly not unbearable.

I remember to this day wanting very much to know she wanted and accepted me. I worked hard to gain that acceptance a hundred different ways. Had she seen me as an extra-special gift from God, my childhood memories would be far more pleasant. As I reached manhood, her respect for and interest in me became evident. But I didn't really need it then—I needed it as a child.

The story about Jabez ends on a bright note:

> Now Jabez called on the God of Israel, saying, "Oh that Thou wouldst bless me indeed, and enlarge my border, and that Thy hand might be with me, and that Thou wouldst keep me from harm, that it may not pain me!" And God granted him what he requested (1 Chron. 4:10).

God overcame that difficult childhood. Jabez was determined not to submerge beneath a sea of negativism. Although his birth struck a minor chord, he trusted God to make his life a major triumph. God did.

I've noticed from this example of Jabez that the unplanned children are occasionally the ones who have the most potential—as if God personally designed them, *determined* to have them born. Leonardo Da Vinci is a case in point. Unplanned and unwanted . . . but what a contribution to humanity!

I suggest you give attention to your attitude toward your unplanned child. It might help if you realize that the child may be unplanned by you . . . but certainly not by God. It's possible that a mother who reads these words is carrying that particular child right now. In a few months, you'll hold him in your arms. You have a choice. You and your husband can accept and love and nurture that little one as God's very special package for a very special purpose. Or you can communicate the opposite.

Your child will know. Believe me, he'll know. He can tell by the way he is held and fed and bathed and dressed. Our tone of voice, even our touch, communicates volumes.

Feel like it's too much to handle? Too intense a situation? Christians find hope in Phil. 4:13:

I have strength for all things in Christ Who empowers me—I am ready for anything and equal to anything through Him Who infuses inner strength into me [that is, I am self-sufficient in Christ's sufficiency] (Amplified Bible).

. . . and Is. 41:10:

Fear not; [there is nothing to fear] for I am with you; do not look around you in terror and be dismayed, for I am your God. I will strengthen and harden you [to difficulties]; yes, I will help you; yes, I will hold you up and retain you with My victorious right hand of rightness and justice (Amplified Bible).

. . . and don't forget Ps. 127:3-4:

Lo, children are a heritage from the Lord, the fruit of the womb a reward. As arrows are in the hand of a warrior, so are the children of one's youth (Amplified Bible).

Share your honest feelings with your mate or a close personal friend. Ask the Lord to change your mindset so you'll be able to love and train His extra-special gift in the years to come. He will hear. He will answer.

THE ADOPTED CHILD

Many who read this book have adopted one or more of your children. Congratulations! You have employed the same method of expanding your family that God uses. In three New Testament chapters—Galatians 4, Ephesians 1, and Romans 8—we find our spiritual adoption explained. Through faith in the Lord Jesus Christ, we are taken by our Father God and placed as sons and daughters into His family. This allows us all the rights and privileges of that new spiritual relationship.

When you adopt a child, you bypass a very significant span of time. I'm referring to that nine-month period of pregnancy when the mother and father have time to think through what is ahead and plan together for it. You also accept the fact that you will be somewhat in the dark regarding the child's heredity. This might complicate your understanding of the child's bents and medical history, as we discussed in Chapter 2. It doesn't pose any overwhelming barrier, but it does call for extra sensitivity on the part of parents. You must be keen and alert as you come to know your adopted child. You haven't the benefit of grandparents who can help you see into your child's bents.

Adopted children should know early in life that they have been adopted. If communicated correctly in those formative years, the child adapts with very little difficulty, usually none. It's been my observation that the adopted child may wrestle with two related feelings as he moves into the teen years, perhaps before.

First, the feeling of insecurity. Second, the feeling that he wasn't wanted . . . which can have a serious effect on his self-esteem. If the lines of communication are kept open with mom and dad, however, such struggles are minimal.

My wife and I became very close friends with a remarkable couple in our church in Massachusetts years ago. Being unable to have their own children, they first adopted a baby boy and some time later a baby girl. The mother of the home had also been adopted as a child, so she had great capacity for understanding her children's needs.

That home was a model of mutual love and profound security. Cynthia and I were admittedly somewhat surprised to discover the children had been adopted. They were, by then, teenagers and just as secure as any adult you'd ever want to meet. I asked the son if he ever wrestled with those inner feelings of insecurity, if he ever wished he had not been adopted. His answer was quick and clever: "No way! In fact, I sorta feel sorry for kids that *weren't* adopted. Their folks had to take what they got . . . but mine got to choose!"

THE HANDICAPPED CHILD

I realize that entire books are written on the subject of handicapped children. There's no way I can undertake an exhaustive treatment of it here, but there are some insights from Scripture that might add understanding and encouragement. By "handicapped" I make reference to congenital birth defects: blindness, deafness, speech defects, a crippled condition in the body, mental retardation, and other damages incurred before or during birth.

Since medicine is not my field, I shall not attempt to present that side of the subject. I will stick exclusively with the Scriptures and base my comments on those truths we uncover. Certainly, if you wish to probe deeper than we are able to go, you should seek the counsel of qualified professionals either personally or in literature.

To begin with, let's look at several verses from the Bible without an interrupting comment.

> Then Moses said to the Lord, "Please, Lord, I have never been eloquent, neither recently nor in time past, nor since Thou hast spoken to Thy servant; for I am slow of speech and slow of tongue." And the Lord said to him, "Who has made man's mouth? Or who makes him dumb or deaf, or seeing or blind? Is it not I, the Lord" (Ex. 4:10-11)?

Next, consider Job's words as he was suffering:

> Thy hands fashioned and made me altogether, And wouldst Thou destroy me? Remember now, that Thou hast made me as clay; And wouldst Thou turn me into dust again? Didst Thou not pour me out like milk, And curdle me like cheese; Clothe me with skin and flesh, And knit me together with bones and sinews? Thou hast granted me life and lovingkindness; and Thy care has preserved my spirit (Job 10:8-12).

And you'll remember this from David's pen:

For Thou didst form my inward parts; Thou didst weave me in my mother's womb. My frame was not hidden from Thee, When I was made in secret, And skillfully wrought in the depths of the earth. Thine eyes have seen my unformed substance; And in Thy book they were all written, The days that were ordained for me, When as yet there was not one of them (Ps. 139:13, 15-16).

Solomon adds:

Just as you do not know the path of the wind and how bones are formed in the womb of the pregnant woman, so you do not know the activity of God who makes all things (Eccles. 11:5).

And Isaiah, an ancient prophet, writes:

Thus says the Lord, your Redeemer, and the one who formed you from the womb, "I, the Lord, am the maker of all things. . . . "(Is. 44:24).

From those marvelous verses of truth, we discover two threads woven through God's plan: (1) God is sovereign over the womb. He takes full responsibility for the changes and alterations that transpire within the fetus. He repeatedly states that He makes us; He forms us. (2) We are limited in our understanding. Our finite minds restrict our grasp of God's plan. We cannot possibly realize why He does what He does nor how it all fits together.

Glance over these words:

Oh, the depth of the riches both of the wisdom and knowledge of God! How unsearchable are His judgments and unfathomable His ways (Rom. 11:33)!

Deep . . . unsearchable . . . unfathomable.

As you hold in your arms today a child who has been born less than what is commonly called "perfect," it is essential that you *view* that child correctly. That will make a world of difference in your attitude toward him and God and yourself. His condition today is not a freak of nature. Mother Nature did not make your child—God did. Remember, He takes full responsibility. I am of the opinion you will never be able to relieve the pressure or overcome the heartache until you see your child as having been made by God.

Another factor that will help you with your attitude is that you finally accept the fact that you may never know why God chose to make your child this way. Parents often search for sin in their own lives, thinking their handicapped child is God's judgment upon them. Or they strive to discover some other hidden reason to explain their circumstance. We cannot fully fathom the Father's plan. It's deep, unsearchable, unfathomable.

The disciples thought a lot like people today. They stood before a man, blind from birth, and asked: ". . . who sinned, this man or his parents, that he should be born blind" (John 9:2)?

Jesus' answer has encouraged many a parent: "It was neither . . . but it was in order that the works of God might be displayed in Him" (John 9:3).

That last comment is simply beautiful. Somehow, some way, at some time in God's great plan, He will "display His works" in your child. He will use your child in your life, in your home, with his friends, in the most amazing ways to display His works. Your extra-special child will become an extra-special object lesson to others. He will be, in fact, a model of specific truths God will communicate to others. And never forget . . . so will his parents.

Quite likely some who read these words have children who were not born handicapped but have become handicapped since then. It is no less an adjustment . . . sometimes it's harder! For your sake I should say the same principles apply. The sovereign God who watched over your child in the womb was there and was still in control when your child suffered his present handicap. God has His infinite inscrutable reasons. He chooses not to reveal them. He understands your turmoil and heartache, the agony of disappointment. But through it all He loves you and has only good in His ultimate plan.

I think of "Joni" who has written her story in her book by that name. Active, vivacious, energetic, and athletic at seventeen, Joni is now paralyzed from her neck down—a twenty-six-year-old paraplegic as a result of a diving accident. But she has learned to draw beautiful pictures by holding the pencil in her mouth. Her art work is in demand all across America. Read her book. You'll be encouraged.

While my family and I were up at Mount Hermon Family Camp last year, God displayed His works to us. An amazing family was among us. Only one of the four children was "normal." Two were dwarfs and a third was born with only one heart valve. The two dwarfs walked with crutches and had to wear braces on their legs. The flesh of the boy with the congenital heart problem was not the normal color, due to poor circulation. No physician understands how he has lived to the age of twelve.

All week long we talked and laughed and played together. They were a delightful family . . . no bitterness, no self-pity, not even the slightest glimmer of irritation. The last day of camp that family walked down in front around the fire and sang together, "We're Something Special." There wasn't a dry eye in the place. God used those three handicapped children and their supportive sister and parents to "display His works" among us. As they sang I got a whole new appreciation for the way God allows families with handicapped children to model His truths.

THE GIFTED CHILD

Occasionally, God gives extra-special children who possess incredible abilities. Some are academically bright, "quiz kids." Others have certain talents that relate to the arts or some other phase of life. Jesus was obviously in this category. At the young age of twelve He displayed how gifted he was. Dr. Luke tells us His parents ". . . found Him in the temple, sitting in the midst of the teachers, both listening to them and asking them questions. And all who heard Him were amazed at His understanding and His answers" (Luke 2:46-47).

In the chapter on the home training Jesus received, we talked about how wise His parents were not to push Him. Perhaps your child, without any push on your part, is showing real promise. Observe that and communicate with your mate to do the same. Your support and encouragement are really all your child needs.

If it's music, don't hold him back. If at all possible, place him under a competent private teacher. Purchase an instrument if that is his interest. The gifted child usually has a built-in motivation, so you won't have to prod him as much as others . . . but there will be occasions where parental control will help him stay on target.

Academically gifted children are frequently moody. Being

bright, they are often moved ahead in school, allowed to skip a grade. This may stimulate them mentally as they are challenged with an accelerated learning situation, but emotionally it's tough for them to handle. Here, parents need to be wise and extremely careful. Your child is more than a brain. He's a whole person. Even though he may be a borderline prodigy, he is *still a child*. Keep that in mind.

Often it's the bright kids that drop out, get into drugs, and slide into the subculture. Invariably, they have lost their emotional balance. That vital relationship between child and parent must be maintained. You may not be able to stay up with them in advanced math or nuclear physics or philosophy, but you can be there to add stability. You can help maintain their equilibrium with solid counsel or just a listening ear.

Experts tell us when a child's brilliance soars to an I.Q. of 180 or more, he is likely to suffer from being "too different." Other kids are cruel. They will freeze out anybody who is "different." Your gifted child will need more help in knowing how to mix with others socially than how to get it together scholastically.

Let me share a final thought on this subject. The super-gifted child will occasionally be a perfectionist. In your eyes his work or accomplishments will seem astounding, but not in *his* eyes. You will see what is done; he will see what is missing. You will be pleased; he won't. Chances are he won't even turn in his work at school if he is too displeased. That perfectionism syndrome, if not handled wisely, could lead to deep problems. Strange as it may seem, the gifted, overly capable child can struggle with a profound sense of inferiority, almost to the point of suicide.

Draw him out. Break through his preoccupation. Do whatever is necessary to keep those lines of communication strong. It may be tough at times, but the alternative is far worse.

THE HYPERACTIVE CHILD

Of all the children who are a challenge to raise, few are more exasperating and demanding than the hyperactive child. Unfortunately, not only are the parents struggling, so is the child.

This particular child may span the extremes between being easily distracted because of a short attention span to being totally uncontrollable. He may not complete his work. He may not remember what you said to him three minutes ago. He may not follow rules and regulations. He may fail to manifest certain kinds of affectionate behavior. He may be impulsive, easily upset, loud, disorderly, and disorganized (untucked shirts, unzipped zippers), and perhaps be a bed-wetter. Of course, displaying any one of these symptoms does not mean your child is hyperactive, but if most persist to an intense degree, it's worth looking into. All these symptoms (and there are many more!) help you understand why the hyperactive child is frequently disobedient.

Let's go back to our scriptural home base, Prov. 22:6:

Train up a child in the way he should go,
Even when he is old he will not depart from it.

We are learning that our training methods are to be in keeping with our child's "way"—his bent, characteristics, and needs. All the way through this book you are encouraged to make a thorough study of your youngster. Why? So your training might be adapted to fit his way.

This is never more important than in the case of a hyperactive child. You, his parent, must remain confident you can handle your child. Your consistent and firm leadership is the key to your child's training. Don't relinquish it under any circumstance. You will be made to feel guilty; some will blame you for causing your child to be hyperactive. You will feel intimidated as professionals suggest you are responsible.

After considerable experience and research in this area, I'm convinced that in virtually all instances hyperactivity is the result of *inborn temperamental differences* in the child. How that child is raised may affect the severity of his problem, but *it is not the cause* of hyperactivity. A child who is not temperamentally predisposed to hyperactivity cannot "catch it" from his parents.

It's amazing to me how tolerant and understanding people can be of parents of the handicapped, yet unbelievably intolerant of parents of the hyperactive. That increases the level of guilt and also robs the confidence of parents. Let's hear from an expert, Dr. Paul H. Wender. This physician is an authority in the field of hyperactivity and his counsel is well worth our attention:

In the recent past almost all child psychiatrists and psychologists have maintained that most of the behavioral problems seen in children were the results of the manner in which they were raised by their parents. Most parents who have done any reading on child rearing are aware of these notions, but are not aware they are becoming very much out of date. Such parents reach what they think is an obvious conclusion: They have a child with behavior difficulties. Children's behavior difficulties are the results of their parents' difficulties. Therefore, the parents—they themselves—must be either stupid or evil. Their child's difficulties are not only a serious problem in themselves, but are also a reflection of the parents' failure as parents. Unfortunately, many mental health workers may reinforce the parents in this view of themselves. A substantial number of psychiatrists, psychologists, social workers, teachers, and school guidance counselors are unaware of the problem of hyperactivity. They, too, believe the child's problems are a reflection of his parents' problems. They will inform the parent, subtly or otherwise, that he is responsible for his child's difficulties. This will either intensify the parent's sense of guilt, anxiety, and depression, or lead him to deny there is anything wrong with his child. The latter course would be difficult to follow, but rather than be labeled as bad parents of a bad child, some people will deny the evidence of their senses and proclaim their child is perfectly normal but misunderstood by others. This is an understandable, common, and unfortunate technique that delays or prevents the problem from being solved. Many parents of HA children have accused themselves for many years, and a final prosecution by experts may lead them to defend themselves by denying the existence of problems in the child, which in turn leads to the child's not receiving treatment. The important point I wish the reader to take away is that, contrary to usual belief, family disturbances are often the result and not the cause of a child's problems.[11]

If you have a hyperactive child, I would suggest you purchase two books: *The Hyperactive Child* by Paul H. Wender, M.D., and *Why Your Child Is Hyperactive* (Random House) by Ben F. Feingold, M.D. They will make excellent companion volumes to help encourage you in raising a hyperactive youngster.

Three final comments are in order:

1. Research the facts. Refuse hearsay or surface diagnosis

or that which "seems plausible." Some very objective and attainable solutions will emerge as you research. Call upon a competent pediatrician or pediatric neurologist who is knowledgeable about the entire range of children's behavioral, physical, and emotional problems, including hyperactivity. There are diagnostic tests that can be performed on your child. Dr. Wender suggests:

> If the child's pediatrician is consulted, the parent should be aware that some pediatricians have little training in dealing with behavior problems. The parent should frankly ask him if he is familiar with behavior problems, and if he is not, whom he could recommend who might be more experienced in this field.[12]

2. Reject guilt. If you listen to others, you will become a victim—a helpless parent without confidence.

3. Remain consistent. The setting of firm, fair rules is absolutely essential. Follow through. Hyperactive children need a more structured environment than other children.

THE SINGLE-PARENT CHILD

Finally, that extra-special child in your home might be growing up with only one parent in authority over him. Death or divorce or a half-dozen other reasons might have brought about the circumstances of your home.

Four suggestions might make your child's life, as well as your own, more enriching.

To begin with, *your positive attitude* toward the one-parent situation is all-important. That child will pick up the same attitude. You cannot fake it nor hide it. At times, kids are virtually omniscient! If you become bitter and resentful, so will he. If you harbor a grudge, somehow he will detect it and emulate it.

This is particularly true in divorce situations where resentments are built into mountainous proportions. This is most unfortunate. Perhaps you cannot live with each other in harmony, but I suggest you make every effort to gain and give the forgiveness of one another so you may be released from the grip of internal bitterness. This will bring freedom into your life, allowing you and your former mate the opportunity to make a mutual contribution to the development of your child.

If you succumb to self-pity and loneliness, be ready for a child who will mirror the same attitude. Ask God for a personal awareness of His presence. Start the day that way. Cultivate an hour-by-hour relationship with your Lord. He cares and He will come to your side in those lonely hours.

Another thought worth considering is *your diligent spirit* to carry through the same principles of raising your child that you would if your mate were there. God's Word gives us guidelines to live by *regardless* of our circumstances. Training techniques, consistent discipline, abundant love, wise counsel—all these must be pursued diligently. You cannot afford to give up!

> Therefore, my beloved brethren, be steadfast, immovable, always abounding in the work of the Lord, knowing that your toil is not in vain in the Lord (1 Cor. 15:58).

That's not just a verse for pastors. It is equally applicable to single parents. Your labor is not in vain. Your child will some day rise up and call you blessed if you give all you've got.

A family in one of my former pastorates comes to my mind. There are seven children in all. Shortly after the birth of the youngest, the father of the family buried his dear wife. The motherless children looked to their daddy for direction—and did he ever give it! They sat in a circle the evening following the funeral and made a covenant with one another to weather the storm, stick together, and never give up.

Today, most are grown. Their lives are sterling examples of the diligent spirit of that brave, determined father. In the words of that verse of Scripture, they were steadfast, immovable, and abounding! I recall few families that had more fun or enjoyed their vacations more than that one.

A third suggestion has to do with *your close friends*. People who live alone (especially single parents) tend to crawl into a self-made shell. That is perhaps the worst thing you can possibly do. Start looking for some wholesome people with whom you can become close friends. You might even discover a family or two with whom you can share your life. Be discerning; as time passes those adults will be models your children will watch and even seek out for counsel.

A healthy by-product of this suggestion is that you will become involved in their lives, helping and loving and ministering to them as well. You might even begin to entertain others in your home or apartment. It's awfully hard to get absorbed in self-pity while we are involved in helping others.

Furthermore, if that friendship is an honest one, they will assist you by telling you the truth about your life and your child's behavior. All of us have blind spots. We need a mate, a parent, or an intimate friend to shed light on the scene. Solomon realized this when he wrote:

> Faithful are the wounds of a friend, But deceitful are the kisses of an enemy . . . . Iron sharpens iron, So one man sharpens another (Prov. 27:6, 17).

A final suggestion for single parents has to do with *your spiritual walk*. I hinted at this in my first suggestion, but let's go further. If ever you needed divine assistance and strength, it's now. Your personal relationship with Jesus Christ is absolutely essential. You will need time in His Word—*regularly*. You should maintain a prayer life on a daily basis. Sharing your faith with others plus attending a church that teaches the Scriptures will do much to enhance your life. Being spiritually on target is a must. Talk about the Lord with your children. Include Him as the special guest at every meal you serve. Your growth in Christ will be a pattern, a testimony to the world around you. The Lord God will magnify His name through you.

If you are attempting to raise your children without a father, this verse of Scripture might bring encouragement: "A father of the fatherless and a judge for the widows, Is God in His holy habitation. God makes a home for the lonely" (Ps. 68:5-6a).

Extra-special children are extra-special gifts from God, calling for extra-special love which will require extra-special insight and wisdom. With the right attitude, a so-called tragedy can be turned into a triumph.

10
Releasing Your Child

Perhaps by now your Bible will automatically open to the book of Proverbs! We've looked at length into this great book of wisdom. We've spent most of our time talking about the first half of Prov. 22:6, the part that deals with knowing, training, loving, and disciplining our children. We've talked a lot about the child's relationship to his parents in the home.

But what about the last part of that verse? That part talks about the relationship of the child to the parents (and their relationship to him) once he's gone from home.

> Train up a child in the way he should go,
> Even when he is old he will not depart from it.

Depart from what? He will not depart from the training, from the personal investment that has been made in his life. Unfortunately, as we have seen, even if the investment has been the wrong kind, he will still not depart from it. More happily, if the investment has been right, he won't depart from that either. The promise is that when the child is old he won't depart from his training.

The word rendered *old* here means, remember, "hair on the chin," or "one who has a beard." Solomon did not mean old in the sense of being ancient or over the hill, but old in the sense of being grown up, mature, adult.

THE HOME: GOD'S IDEA

It is significant to me that some of the first things God ever said to man had to do with the home. This tells us something of God's priority list.

> And God created man in His own image, in the image of God He created him; male and female He created them. And God blessed them; and God said to them, "Be fruitful and multiply,

and fill the earth, and subdue it, and rule over the fish of the sea and over the birds of the sky, and over every living thing that moves on the earth" (Gen. 1:27-28).

God said to the very first couple, the very first married pair on earth, "I'm concerned about populating the earth. I'm interested that you live with reproduction in mind."

Obviously, God did not intend for Adam and Eve to fill the whole earth themselves. He also refers to their children and their children's children, right up to today.

Equally obvious, in order for man to be raised up, to reproduce, he must be released from his parents. Just across the page in Gen. 2:24, God deals with that issue. The very next time He addresses man, He says,

> For this cause a man shall leave his father and his mother, and shall cleave to his wife [the Hebrew word conveys the idea of "glueing" himself to his wife]; and they shall become one flesh.

There is to be an inseparable bonding of the two when they become one.

God told the first couple to be fruitful and multiply and fill the earth. When He addressed them again, He said that in order for couples to have this kind of intimacy and relationship they must leave father and mother. That doesn't mean to abandon them or ignore them and forget you ever had them. It means you move out from under their wing. There is to be a shift of authority. Both sets of parents are to take "hands off" as a new home begins.

A great frustration often comes when we release our children. In one sense, it is natural for this period of release to be difficult. In another sense, we make it hard on ourselves.

First of all, I want to discuss the reasons why it is abnormally difficult for us to release our children. Then toward the end of the chapter I want to talk about things to keep in mind that will make the release easier.

Why is releasing your child difficult? God gave you your child, as we saw in Chapters 1 and 2, with a particular set of prescribed tendencies or bents. He has an evil bent from a *general* point of view which he received through his connection with the human race because of sin. He got his from you. You got yours from your parents. And it goes all the way back to Adam.

We have likewise learned your child also has an evil bent in a *specific* sense that he picked up from you and from your parents and your grandparents. We looked at length at the case of Abraham, and his tendency toward lying.

More importantly, each child has particular tendencies toward good. The parent who builds the child according to these bents will enhance these qualities, enabling the child to become his own person in God's kingdom. In other words, he will be training up a child according to the child's own way as created by God. This is the parent's *primary responsibility.*

WHY RELEASE COMES HARD

The first reason for difficulty in releasing a child comes when parents build *themselves* into their children rather than developing the child according to how *God* designed him. When we do this either purposefully or inadvertently, we go through terrible feelings at the time of release. Why? Because a measure of our identity is being passed on. We are, in effect, losing something of ourselves. That's painful.

The father who was not able to become an accomplished musician, for example, or attain other artistic achievements can suffer a lot of inner struggle when his musical son leaves the nest. Part of the father's desires have begun to be lived out in the boy. When release time comes, the father thinks, "I don't want to let him go."

The mother who was terribly frustrated as a child sees in her child the opportunity to build those things she lacked. When it comes time for the daughter to leave on the day of her wedding, mom goes through definite withdrawal pains, because part of her goes that day too. The Lord guards us against this when He tells us to "train up a child in the way he should go [according to his way]. . . ."

In other words, one of the most difficult things for a parent to do is to remain objective. Fight like an enemy this subjective tendency of pouring into your children the things you always wanted to become in life. If you don't, you'll be crying at their wedding for the wrong reason.

The second cause for a difficult release involves a quick review of Eph. 5:22-33. These twelve verses give instructions for the home. You are probably familiar with them because this passage is often read at weddings. God discusses the home in this text by talking with the husbands and the wives. He doesn't talk to children.

Wives, be subject to your own husbands. . . . (v. 22).

Husband, love your wives. . . . (v. 25).

Husbands ought also to love their own wives as their own bodies. . . . (v. 28).

Nevertheless let each individual among you also love his own wife even as himself; and let the wife see to it that she respects her husband. . . . (v. 33).

I make a major point out of this because *children are never mentioned here*. Why? Because *children were never designed to be the weld that holds the home together!*

This explains the second reason parents often find great difficulty in releasing their children: the parental relationship has become stronger than the marriage relationship. The child has been put into a role he was never designed to fit. Thus, when it's time for the child to be released, it becomes evident that the parents have used their children as the glue to keep their marriage together through tremendous difficulty.

It is interesting to me that the national divorce rate forms a graph that resembles a "V" as far as time is concerned. Broken marriages hit a high peak in their early years when the relationship is shaky. When children come, divorce slacks off. Responsibility brings a stark realization: "I can't leave. I've got to raise these kids and it's impossible to do it alone." Out of guilt, the couples stay together. During that time the glue sets. Hard as cold concrete.

Then, about the time the children leave home, the rate skyrockets almost off the graph. Something else happens. Insecure parents, who found in their children what they should have found in their mates, cannot cope with the release. They have lost the single thread that tied them to happiness. The release becomes cause for mourning.

Wives and husbands, are you establishing a relationship that revolves around your children or around your mate? It is terribly unfortunate to put a child in the position of holding the home together. Husbands, do you *love* your wives? Tell them! Show them.

This is why I advocate getting alone periodically just as husband and wife. That's important. Get alone and revive what has been lacking. Get back into that delightful love relationship. If you dodge it and ignore it long enough, it will take its toll in your life. And further, when you come to those days—whether it's college, marriage, or career—when your child says, "That's it, folks. I'd really like to go it on my own," tremendous emotional damage will await in the wings.

The first reason it is difficult to release a child comes because parents build themselves into the child, and the second is a result of the parental relationship becoming stronger than the marital relationship.

The third reason for a difficult release is unveiled in 2 Cor. 12:14, where Paul is writing to a church he dearly loves. He says,

> Here for this third time I am ready to come to you, and I will not be a burden to you; for I do not seek what is yours, but you; for children are not responsible to save up for their parents, but parents for their children.

What he means is that he won't reach into their hip pockets. It's a diplomatic, ecclesiastical way of saying, "I'm not coming for money. I come not for your support, but for *you*."

The principle here is that children do not serve the parents, but parents serve the children. We touched on this same verse earlier, you may recall. The application we can make here is that people do not have children because they *need* them but because they *want* them. Children are the by-products of love between a husband and a wife.

Let's go back to the application of 2 Cor. 12:14. It is not the child who supports the parents; the parents support the child. (And that certainly includes more than money.) Paul wrote to Timothy,

> But if any one does not provide for his own, and especially for those of his household, he has denied the faith, and is worse than an unbeliever (1 Tim. 5:8).

Look at 2 Cor. 12:15:

And I will most gladly spend and be expended for your souls. If I love you the more, am I to be loved the less?

The third reason for difficulty in releasing children is clear in this passage. Release of the child will be traumatic for parents who possess an abnormal, unhealthy *need* for the child, as opposed to a normal, loving, unselfish relationship.

Do you know who really has to battle with this? My heart goes out to them—the single parents who raise the family. We talked about this difficult situation in Chapter 9. If death or divorce has come and the child is raised by one parent, that parent can easily develop an inordinate need for the child. There often comes to pass a relationship far too strong for the child (or parent) to handle correctly. We shouldn't build ourselves into our children, except in the sense of discipleship. Remember that. We need to allow them the freedom to become the people God intended.

Wise, sensitive parents spend years helping their children reach their full potential. This does two things, both of which are healthy and wholesome. First, it helps the parent loosen the ties. Month by month, year after year, as the process occurs the parent is releasing—slowly but surely. Stronger expressions of independence are heard from the child. Sensitive parents interpret those sounds correctly. They are in the process of letting them go. That's all part of being unselfish.

Second, it helps the youngster stretch his wings without fear of getting them clipped. A context of secure, loving freedom is his to enjoy. He's eager to become himself as a person. He's not made to feel guilty because he enjoys the process. And when the final day of release arrives, he's ready and so are his parents. Tears may flow—but those are joyful tears!

PREPARING FOR RELEASE

Let's turn from the problems to the solutions. What should we do to prepare for the time of release? Assuming you have a relationship with your child such that you don't try to live your life out through him; assuming you have a relationship with your spouse that is stronger than with the child; assuming you are developing your child's life not because you need him but because he needs you, let's move on.

Ecclesiastes 2:18-20 contains some very strong words from a

man who was looking at life from strictly a horizontal, earthly point of view:

> Thus I hated all the fruit of my labor for which I had labored under the sun, for I must leave it to the man who will come after me. [Some of us dads will groan on that verse.] And who knows whether he will be a wise man or a fool? Yet he will have control over all the fruit of my labor for which I have labored by acting wisely under the sun. This too is vanity. Therefore, I completely despaired of all the fruit of my labor for which I had labored under the sun [Why? Because—] When there is a man who has labored with wisdom, knowledge and skill, then he gives his legacy to one who has not labored with them. This too is vanity and a great evil.

The Living Bible renders a couple of those verses like this:

> Who can tell whether my son will be a wise man or a fool, and yet all I have will be given to him. How discouraging! I must leave all of it to someone who hasn't done a day's work in his life, and he inherits all my labors and efforts free of charge. This is not only foolish, but unfair.

Now what is the principle we are after in this passage? *Children should be trained to handle their parents' legacy.* Releasing a child does not mean we give him life on a silver platter. Please remember: Getting something for nothing breeds irresponsibility. Children sometimes hate to hear this kind of instruction, but it's the truth. By the time they leave the nest, grown children must have developed a proper scale of values. It's one of the basics of life. It's like a rudder on a ship. Without it you're flirting with disaster.

This father described in Ecclesiastes 2 has labored in his enterprise—lived with it, nurtured it, and cultivated it. Tension and pressure made it a hell on earth at times, but he's babied it and sacrificed for it and finally gets it off the runway. The enterprise begins to grow and before long it has become something beautiful to behold in its fruitfulness.

But sooner than he expected the years have gone by and the father has to bail out. He has to turn it over to that son of his.

The business was airborne, but the son has never been taught to fly. He grabs the stick and says, "So long, Dad." CRASH! The son never learned how to handle it. Why? Because he never labored for it. He never learned from his father the disciplines involved that lead to a successful and profitable business.

It's a big pill to swallow, parents, but if that happens, it's more our fault than Junior's! We had twenty years to build responsibility into him.

There is another passage which relates to this in a little book called Lamentations. You perhaps have quoted the verse and maybe never knew where it was found. Lamentations 3:27: "It is good for the man that he should bear the yoke in his youth." It is good, profitable, healthy, and right for a man to carry some responsibility during his growing-up years. In other words, a key role of the parent is to stretch the child, to challenge him so when he gets to the hard places alone, he knows what it's like to hang in there.

Solomon writes, "If you are slack in the day of distress, Your strength is limited" (Prov. 24:20).

Jeremiah agrees.

If you have run with footmen and they have tired you out, Then how can you compete with horses? If you fall down in a land of peace, How will you do in the thicket of the Jordan (Jer. 12:5)?

What do those verses mean to a parent preparing to release children? If your growing youngster can't cut it at home in such things as cleaning up his room, making his bed, and earning part of his own way by the time of maturity, what on earth will he do when he faces a business career and marriage and the pressures of life?

You know, as I write these things I have to be honest and admit to a pang of guilt in my heart, because in my home I was the baby in a family of three children. Like many families who spoil the last, my parents relaxed the discipline a little more than usual. I remember buying my first car, a little Chevrolet. My dad helped me buy it. It came with bad tires, so he paid for the new ones. I burned rubber all over Houston—out of the driveway, on the way to church, at intersections, in the parking lot, around the schoolyard—playing the role . . . big man with his car.

About five months later, those tires were as slick as the top of Kojak's head. I rotated them, even prayed over them, and they just got slicker. So I came to my dad and said, "You know, Pop, the car is doing great, but the tires are gone."

"Is that right?" he said.

"Yeah."

"Well, you'd better get another set."

"No, you don't understand. I don't have any money."

"Well, you'd better save your money."

It's remarkable what that last statement did to my driving. I was working as a machinist at that time, and it took me two and a half months until I finally could afford new tires for that car. And I don't remember ever burning rubber again.

Responsibility helps cure bad habits! And I mean fast. You don't drop transmissions on the highway when you buy your own transmissions. You stop dragging your heels when you buy your own shoes. Children must *learn* to handle life—it does not come naturally. It is good that the child bears a yoke in his youth.

Some of you have built businesses from scratch. You started with nothing. You had nothing. You've turned hard work into something extremely impressive. You have every reason, by the grace of God, to be proud of your labor. Be *very* careful about transferring your labors into the lily-white hands of so-called "good" sons and daughters. It could be, as the Scripture says, vanity and emptiness. Get them ready for it now. You'll be happy later.

One more word along this line . . . do you have a child in college? If so, are you paying everything? You answer, "Sure, why not?" I'm sorry to hear that. Give him the *privilege* of helping with the cost. There is something about an education that makes it altogether more enjoyable, appreciated, and effective when that boy or girl has had to do some work to sustain it.

Okay, before you throw stones at me, let's look at Proverbs 23. The second guideline in releasing your children is to *keep on communicating with them after they leave.*

I've heard a number of mothers say at a daughter's wedding: "Well, I've said all I'm going to say."

Occasionally I ask, "Why?" Perhaps it would be better to ask the bride. It's easy to convey to our parents a resistance to their counsel when we leave home. There's nothing in Scripture that says marriage and communication with parents are mutually exclusive. "Leaving father and mother" does not mean shutting them out. If parents are wise and helpful before marriage, they are the same afterwards, aren't they?

Hear Prov. 23:22-23:

Listen to your father who begot you, And do not despise your mother when she is old. Buy truth, and do not sell it, Get wisdom and instruction and understanding.

Then, verse 26 teaches:

Give me your heart, my son, And let your eyes delight in my ways.

For all we know, the son in the writer's mind may have been married and the father of several children.

Your father was wise when you were fourteen? I'll guarantee you he is wiser when you are twenty-four, and chances are he's far wiser when you're forty-four. But a word of wisdom is in order for moms and dads. The *way* we communicate our counsel is extremely important. It's an art to remain friends with your children after they're married.

A dear lady friend, one whom I deeply respect for the way her children have turned out, shared with me her feelings about releasing her children. She wrote this note:

Mothers have the most difficulty with this phase of our children's life cycle, I believe. They are the nesters and sometimes the smotherers, while dads are of necessity the providers. The first child to leave, whether it be for college, career, or marriage, gives the greatest jolt emotionally. The old apron strings resist being loosened.

But God intended our children to be their own persons, and the greatest favor we can do them is to let them go. The reward of keeping hands off, so to speak, and letting our children be truly *released* is that such a parent, without asking for it, gains his adult children's friendship as well as his love. That is a very special joy. I know. It worked for us.

The very special relationship we now have with our adult children provides us a continuing glow with which to warm our hearts in the home where they no longer live.

It's almost like a fairy tale, isn't it? But it's real. That's the way God has arranged it. I can hardly think of an exception to this observation: The young men and women who enter adulthood with confidence are the ones who were taught by their parents how to handle the issues of life—and they are the ones whose moms and dads are available, waiting in the wings to give counsel or support or assistance whenever it is needed and requested.

Next, *look upon release as a process rather than a sudden event*. You don't release your child the day of his marriage. You begin the process of releasing your child on the day of his birth. You plan on it. You anticipate it. Some days you wish it would hurry up!

Psalm 144:12 refers to the people of Israel and the beauty of their children as they are reared. "Let our sons in their youth be as grown-up plants. [Look at that! Even in their youth, let those boys be looked upon as grown plants.] And our daughters as corner pillars fashioned as for a palace."

In my New American Standard Bible there is a marginal reference: "Let our daughters as corner pillars be *cut after the pattern of a palace*." What a beautiful expression!

I see in the psalmist's words that young men in our homes are to be viewed early by the parents as grown up. And we are to fashion and develop in our daughters the grace and charm and beauty that would enhance the pillars in the temple of God. We are to see our children as "little men" and "little women." I am not suggesting that we not allow our children to be children, but rather that they be challenged to reach their full potential gradually. Look upon release as a process, not something that abruptly occurs on a day in June when you give her hand in marriage. Or that "infamous day" they move into their own apartment. Plan on it.

It's like holding a rope attached to a little skiff in an inlet of a bay. You let the rope out until the skiff begins to feel the movement of the sea. You hold firmly for a while, then you let it out a little further. You still grasp the rope, but it's far enough out for the skiff to be away from you. By and by the rope is tossed. You may watch the skiff in the distance, but you have no control over it.

There is a necessary and normal process of releasing our children into the sea of life. Occasionally, that release may not be as *we* would have planned it. Consider the father in the familiar story of the prodigal son. I'm not the first to observe the absence of a struggle when the son decided to leave home. The father let him go. He knew his boy and was not shocked when the day of departure came. Though no doubt disappointed and unhappy with his son's motive, the father didn't make a scene. He willingly and quietly released his son. You'll also remember he was there when the son decided to return.

The final principle in the process of releasing our children is this: *Engage in the ministry of continual prayer.* I haven't tacked that on to be religious. You know, "Oh, and let's not forget prayer. We want to be sure to pray for our children." Not that at all!

I'm talking about concerted, definite, specific prayer on the part of parents for their children. Job 1:1-5 shows how Job did this with his adult children—which to me explains why he enjoyed such a dynamic relationship with them.

There was a man in the land of Uz, whose name was Job, and that man was blameless, upright, fearing God, and turning away from evil. And seven sons and three daughters were born to him. His possessions also were 7,000 sheep, 3,000 camels, 500 yoke of oxen, 500 female donkeys, and very many servants; and that man was the greatest of all the men of the east. And his sons used to go and hold a feast in the house of each one on his day, and they would send and invite their three sisters to eat and drink with them. And it came about, when the days of feasting had completed their cycle, that Job would send and consecrate them, rising up early in the morning and offering burnt offerings according to the number of them all; for Job said, "Perhaps my sons have sinned and cursed God in their hearts." Thus Job did continually.

That last sentence is the most impressive of all. He did that continually. He stayed at it. Job was a man of prayer. And his prayer life was centered upon the needs of his ten children, now grown.

Susanna Wesley is another illustration of this. She bore nineteen children, although she lost several as infants. I understand by the reading of her biography that Mrs. Wesley gave an hour a week to each child while they were in the home. Uninterrupted time, as best as she could manage it, an hour a week. That alone seems incredible when you think of the demands of meals and clothing and all the needs of growing children. But the amazing part is that when the children left home to strike out for themselves, she invested that same hour during the week in prayer for that child! Where is that kind of parental prayer today?

How do we pray? Well, let's talk about your oldest son. What are his greatest needs right now—one, two, three, four, five? What's your daughter struggling with? What's on her heart these days? What are the issues of life that are really throwing your children a curve? *That's* what we remember for them in prayer. And that's what will enable you to handle the loss. You can turn the problem of releasing into the project of interceding.

I cannot be convinced that any kind of major wedge can be driven between a parent and a child when there is that kind of concern. God is not like that. Prayer cushions the jolt of release.

In the conclusion of this chapter let's review the essential principles by drawing some spiritual analogies. God does not give His children life on a silver platter. Recall the "testimony times" where people have shared the trouble and suffering they've faced as God's children, and how those hard times have been vital to their spiritual growth. We all know it's unrealistic to tell a person, "Receive Christ and all your problems will be over."

God does not stop communicating with His children after they are mature sons and daughters. As a matter of fact, the longer we walk with Him, the *more* we hear from Him! And the *clearer* we hear.

Another thing I've been impressed with is how God continues to stretch us. He looks upon releasing us as a process. Little by little He entrusts us with more and more responsibility. As a very gracious Father, He gives us "just enough rope to hang ourselves," as someone has said, that He might deliver us to adulthood. Growing up is indeed painful.

You see, we're like small children. After crawling like a baby, we learn to walk. After learning to walk, His longer rope allows us to run. Running develops our spiritual muscles and almost before we know it, we realize He sees us as adult sons and daughters.

Last of all, God's Son, the Lord Jesus Christ (our elder brother, the first-born of all creation) keeps on interceding for us from the throne. When everyone else in all the world has taken you off their prayer list, Jesus Christ still prays for you—twenty-four hours a day.

What an unspeakable joy to be in that family whose Father knows us, loves us, trains us, disciplines us, and releases us in the freedom of His constant care!

There is no better place to be on the face of the earth.

11
Hope for the Hurting

In his book, *The Terminal Generation*, Hal Lindsey states:

Man can live about 40 days without food, about 3 days without water, about 8 minutes without air .. but only about 1 second without hope.[13]

You have been reading about raising children God's way. You have thought and smiled and reflected and laughed and maybe even sighed and cried. That's all part of personally interacting with the words on a page as you identify with what you read.

However, some of you are now wrestling with feelings of great disappointment. Perhaps *despair* is a better word. You've raised your children and they are gone. The nest is empty. So is your heart. Because—in all honesty—you blew it. You broke most of the rules, you failed the test, and you cannot go back and try again. The hurt deep within is guilt mixed with a loss of hope. And, as Lindsey reminds us, you can't live very long without hope.

I understand.

And because I do, I want to dedicate these last few pages to you who have a desperate need for hope. And again, I want to base my words on an ancient principle tucked away in the Old Testament.

The passage of Scripture that applies so perfectly to your situation is found in the little book of Joel. In a series of several verses toward the end of the second chapter, God promised hope to people whose crops, groves, and vineyards had been ruined by insects. So severe was the damage that many of the trees and vines would remain fruitless for years. The bleak branches would hang limp and unproductive . . . a pathetic scene! But in the midst of that hopeless condition, the voice of God penetrated. Consider the hope that accompanied His promises:

And the threshing floors will be full of grain, And the vats will overflow with the new wine and oil. "Then I will make up to you for the years that the swarming locust has eaten, the creeping locust, The stripping locust, and the gnawing locust, My great army which I sent among you. And you shall have plenty to eat and be satisfied, And praise the name of the Lord your God, Who has dealt wondrously with you; Then My people will never be put to shame. Thus you will know that I am in the midst of Israel, And that I am the Lord your God and there is no other; And My people will never be put to shame" (Joel 2:24-26).

Allow me to lift a statement from that section of Scripture and apply it to your home.

. . . I will make up to you for the years that the swarming locust has eaten . . . .

The locust of parental neglect and insensitivity may have taken its toll on your children's lives years ago. The swarming insects of indifference or ignorance or impatience or a host of other famines brought on by your failures ate away at your relationship with those precious children, resulting today in barrenness and perhaps even bitterness and resentment on their part.

Now they are grown. You cannot relive those years. That's a fact.

But God can *renew* them. That's a promise! That's *hope*!

If He was able to "make up for the years" locusts devoured the crops of Judah, then He is certainly able to do the same for you with your family—even though it may seem impossible. God is a Specialist in impossible situations. He is the Physician who can bring internal healing. He specializes in binding up fractured relationships and healing deep wounds and bruises that have existed for years. In the words of Isaiah, another prophet:

And if you give yourself to the hungry, And satisfy the desire of the afflicted, Then your light will rise in darkness, And your gloom will become like midday. And the Lord will continually guide you, And satisfy your desire in scorched places, And give strength to your bones; And you will be like a watered garden, And like a spring of water whose waters do not fail. And those from among you will rebuild the ancient ruins; You will raise up the age-old foundations; And you will be called the repairer of the breach, The restorer of the streets in which to dwell (Isa. 58:10-12).

Personalize those words. Think about the children you may have injured or bruised. They have been, in the words of the prophet, "afflicted." That affliction, like vineyards after the locusts leave, may seem too deep for healing ever to occur. They may appear permanently damaged. Not so.

God promises hope. He assures you He can step in and "guide . . . satisfy your desire . . . give strength . . . rebuild ruins . . . repair the breach . . . and restore" the darkness and scorched places.

What does He ask of you? He simply asks you to "give yourself" (Isa. 58:10). As a parent who has blown it, the best place to start is with *an open, honest confession of failure before God and before your children*. That's the place to begin "giving yourself."

If they are near, do so face to face. If not, a phone call or letter would be the next best approach. Hold nothing back. Express the agony of your soul, the depth of remorse you feel, the guilt with which you can no longer cope, the wrong for which you are responsible. Choosing your words carefully, humbly ask your child to forgive you. Refuse any attempt to justify your previous actions. Speak slowly, calmly, and quietly.

I must mention that you should be braced for any response. That offended child, now grown, has lived with the consequences for years. He may burst forth with a blast against you . . . or find himself so shocked he will be stunned and silent. It may take a while for the two of you to work through or negotiate the forgiveness process. An offended individual often finds it difficult to be won back. Listen to Prov. 18:19:

A brother offended is harder to be won than a strong city,
And contentions are like the bars of a castle.

Restrain putting words in his mouth or forcing the transaction. Let him think it through at his own pace. Stay quiet. Pray in your mind. Healing will begin as your child verbally states his willingness to accept your apology and forgive you. It may take time.

Please try not to be afraid of humbling yourself before your child. Hopefully he will soon begin to replace resentment with respect. With some, I repeat, it will take more time . . . but God can pull it off. Remember, He promises to make up for the barren years. Claim that great principle! Count on Him to create and cultivate fruitful changes within your children's hearts. You "give yourself" and then trust God to do His part.

Following this you may find your child beginning to open up to your counsel. You may then start to cultivate a relationship.

Another suggestion that will encourage you is this: *Begin building into the lives of your grandchildren*. How strategic is the role of grandparents!

As I was growing up, my most pleasant memories go back to the treasured hours I spent with my "granddaddy" in South Texas. That man knew me and loved me like no one else on earth. Being with him was the fulfillment of my dearest childhood dreams. To this day I recall his wise counsel, his godly perspective on life, his keen sense of humor, his generous spirit, his common-sense approach to problems, and his frequent, warm, affectionate embraces. I respected him as though he never made a mistake. My life was immeasurably enriched by him. The day of his death was one of the most difficult experiences I ever endured. I live in the legacy of his personal investments.

A sad reflection of our times is seen in the lack of emphasis we place upon the role of grandparents. Try not to let it happen to you. Reach out and "give yourself" to those grandkids. Since you may not have known your child or loved and trained your child as you should have, do so with your grandchild. Often the Scriptures speak of seeing one's children's children and delighting in their ways. Remember, Timothy's grandmother Lois invested in her grandson's life to such an extent that Paul refers to her in 2 Tim. 1:5. You will find a refreshing return of hope as you make such an investment.

A final thought worth considering comes to my mind from the last part of an unusual book in the Bible—Ecclesiastes. I referred to this book in my chapter on "You and Your Son," and I'd like to draw a concluding principle from it here.

As Solomon closes his journal, he steps into the future and pictures himself as an old man . . . alone and weak. Then with a view toward that inevitable "finale," he writes a warning in Chapter 11 that is not be be forgotten:

Cast your bread on the surface of the waters, for you will find it after many days. Divide your portion to seven, or even to eight, for you do not know what misfortune may occur on the earth. If the clouds are full, they pour out rain upon the earth; and whether a tree falls toward the south or toward the north, wherever the tree falls, there it lies. He who watches the wind will not sow and he who looks at the clouds will not reap. Just as you do not know the path of the wind and how bones are formed in the womb of the pregnant woman, so you do not know the activity of God who makes all things. Sow your seed in the morning, and do not be idle in the evening, for you do not know whether morning or evening sowing will succeed, or whether both of them alike will be good (Eccles. 11:1-6).

Solomon advises you to *stay active and involved in the lives of others.* You are admonished to "give yourself" to the needs of others. The worst possible thing you can do as one who failed in past years is to hide yourself, lick your wounds, cultivate a self-pity mentality, and pine away your remaining years on earth. Sure, you've failed. Sure, you should have done better. Of course, you feel badly about those years of the swarming locust. But today is the beginning point for your remaining years on earth. Both your family and friends represent people who still need things only you can offer. That's all part of "casting your bread on the water" and "dividing your portion" and "sowing your seed," as Solomon puts it.

The alternative? You know it better than I. A life of endless sorrow, continual bad memories, constant introspection, a guilty or—at best—somber outlook on the rest of your years. That's no way to live!

People who stay in touch and involved with their family and friends are those who stop existing and start living 365 days a year. It is *essential* that you not curl up in a dark corner of society because you have failed. Hold your head up and claim God's promise of hope. Fix your eyes on His Son, Jesus Christ, and count on Him to forgive what you may have done and heal those you may have wounded.

I know of nothing more effective to give lasting hope both to you and your child.

Footnotes

1. Joe Temple, *Know Your Child* (Grand Rapids: Baker Book House, 1974).
2. *Newsweek*, September 22, 1975, "The Parent Gap," pp. 48-56.
3. James Dobson, *Hide or Seek* (Old Tappan, New Jersey: Fleming H. Revell, 1974), p. 51.
4. Thomas C. Short, "Christian Marriage," *Pulpit Digest*.
5. Phi Delta Kappan, May, 1970, "A Scientist Looks at LOVE," pp. 464-465.
6. Kenneth Gangel, *The Family First* (Minneapolis: His International Service, 1972), pp. 134-136.
7. Henry R. Brandt, *Build a Happy Home with Discipline* (Wheaton, Illinois: Scripture Press, Inc., 1960), p. 2.
8. Rebecca Lamar Harmon, *Susanna, Mother of the Wesleys* (Nashville: Abingdon Press, 1968), pp. 58-59.
9. Josiah Gilbert Holland, "God Give Us Men!" *The Best Loved Poems of the American People* (Garden City: Garden City Books, 1936), p. 132.
10. From "You're Something Special," words by William J. and Gloria Gaither and music by William J. Gaither. Copyright© 1974 by William J. Gaither. International copyright secured. All rights reserved. Made in the U.S.A. and used by permission, (as recorded by The Bill Gaither Trio on Impact Records, R-3214, "Especially For Children").
11. Paul H Wender, M.S., *The Hyperactive Child–A Handbook for Parents* (New York: Crown Publishers, Inc., 1973), pp. 44-45.
12. Ibid., p. 110.
13. Hal Lindsey, *The Terminal Generation* (Old Tappan, New Jersey: Fleming H. Revell, 1976), p. 10.